THE EVERYTHING KIDS' MONEY BOOK

SECOND EDITION

Earn it, save it, and watch it grow!

Brette McWhorter Sember, J.D.

A adams media

Avon, Massachusetts

PUBLISHER Karen Cooper

DIRECTOR OF ACQUISITIONS AND INNOVATION Paula Munier

MANAGING EDITOR, EVERYTHING SERIES Lisa Laing

COPY CHIEF Casey Ebert

ACQUISITIONS EDITOR Katie McDonough

DEVELOPMENT EDITOR Elizabeth Kassab

EDITORIAL ASSISTANT Hillary Thompson

An Everything® Series Book.
Everything® and everything.com® are registered trademarks of F+W Media, Inc.

Published by Adams Media, a division of F+W Media, Inc.
57 Littlefield Street, Avon, MA 02322. U.S.A.
www.adamsmedia.com

ISBN-10: 1-59869-784-6
ISBN-13: 978-1-59869-784-1

Printed by R. R. Donnelley, Harrisonburg, VA, USA.

December, 2011

10   9   8   7   6   5   4

This publication is designed to provide accurate and authoritative information with regard to the subject matter covered. It is sold with the understanding that the publisher is not engaged in rendering legal, accounting, or other professional advice. If legal advice or other expert assistance is required, the services of a competent professional person should be sought.
—From a *Declaration of Principles* jointly adopted by a Committee of the American Bar Association and a Committee of Publishers and Associations

Many of the designations used by manufacturers and sellers to distinguish their products are claimed as trademarks. When those designations appear in this book and Adams Media was aware of a trademark claim, the designations have been printed with initial capital letters.

Cover illustrations by Dana Regan.
Interior illustrations by Kurt Dolber.
Puzzles by Scot Ritchie.

This book is available at quantity discounts for bulk purchases.
For information, please call 1-800-289-0963.

Visit the entire Everything® series at *www.everything.com*

CONTENTS

The EVERYTHING KIDS' Money Book

Dedication

For Quinne and Zayne. With one who loves to save and one who loves to spend, I have the best of both worlds!

INTRODUCTION

Money is an exciting thing that is a huge a part of everyday life for kids and grown-ups. You can save it, earn it, spend it, collect it, or just count it. If you're interested in money, there's a lot you can learn. In fact, there's so much it fills this whole book!

Money has a long, long history. Long before there were bills and coins, people used shells and grain as money. ("How much is that?" "That'll be three shells." Can you imagine?) This book has lots of cool facts about money all throughout history. You'll also learn how money is made and what all the marks on money mean. Some money is actually worth more than it says—that's why learning about coin collecting is a great way to discover some extra value in your money! You'll discover what the biggest bill ever made in the United States was worth, how to earn virtual money online, and ideas for what to do with your allowance.

There's more to money than the currency itself, though! Banks, loans, earning money, paying taxes on money, earning interest on money, budgeting, and giving to charity are all super-important ways that money plays a part in your life and the life of your family. Ever wondered how the stock market works? How a bank makes a profit? Have you ever thought about why things cost what they do and why prices go up over time? Were you ever curious about what types of money are used in other countries?

You're about to learn all of that and tons more, such as ways to earn extra dough, how to use gift cards, how a school debit card works, how credit cards work, and how to open and use a bank account. Being smart about money is not just something adults need to do—kids can learn to be wise savers, careful spenders, and smart consumers, too.

Along the way, you'll learn neat facts, awesome tricks, and rad things to do with money!

Chapter 1
THE STORY OF MONEY

Daily Trades

What kinds of trades do you make? You probably make lots of trades without realizing it. If you take out the garbage in order to earn your allowance, you're trading your hard (and smelly!) work for cash. If you buy an action figure at the toy store, you trade dollars for the toy.

TRADE YA!

If you've ever traded the banana from your lunch for someone else's apple, then you've taken part in one of the oldest forms of buying and selling—bartering. Bartering works fairly well as long as the goods being exchanged have the same value, like the apple and the banana. But, what if you wanted to trade a bicycle? How many bananas would equal one bicycle? Probably too many for you to think about without feeling queasy!

How Bartering Worked

Thousands of years ago, people traded with each other on a small scale—one farmer's grapes for another's pumpkins. This worked for a while, but as life became more complex so did the system of bartering. Some people did not farm. They developed other skills such as tool making or basket weaving.

A basket maker may want to buy some grapes, but the farmer already has enough baskets and won't make a trade. A toolmaker needs a basket, so he asks the basket maker to trade for a knife. The basket maker now has a knife that he takes to the farmer to see if the farmer will accept it in exchange for grapes. He will, and the trade is made—but what an uncertain business it is! The poor basket maker could have just as easily ended up without any grapes! And what if the basket maker needed only a few grapes for his lunch? Could the knife have been divided up into smaller pieces? Not if it was to retain its value! Bartering got to be very complicated and time consuming!

BEFORE MONEY THERE WERE COMMODITIES

People needed a better way to do business. Commodity money! Commodity money is when things people commonly had (commodities) were used as money. Barley is an example of a grain that was used for trade. Everyone accepted barley as payment. The basket maker would take barley in return for a basket. The farmer would take the barley for grapes. The toolmaker would take the barley in trade for a knife. Business could be done more efficiently, but people still had to haul big baskets of barley around. Can you imagine if you had to carry a big old basket of barley into the mall to buy something? It wouldn't be easy!

Barley also had its problems. It could spoil or become infested with bugs (eww!). If the barley harvest was poor one year, then there would be very little to use in trade. And there was the problem of transporting it! Another change was needed. Perishable money was replaced by a harder form of money.

Real Money

People next began to use tokens that stood for something of value, such as shells or rocks. The invention of currency, or hard money, required a considerable amount of trust. People had to trust each other to agree on the value of the money.

If all the people in a village decide that five blue pebbles are equal to one chicken and thirty blue pebbles are equal to one goat, then an active trade can be set up using blue pebbles as money. Based upon the price of a chicken, the villagers decide that a bowl of corn is worth one pebble. As long as everyone who is involved agrees, then the village can have a blue pebble currency.

Why did the villagers choose blue pebbles? For two reasons: their beauty and their rarity. Blue pebbles are found only at the back of a deep, dark, scary cave fifty miles away in the mountains. If the villagers had chosen white pebbles, they wouldn't have worked as currency because white pebbles are found everywhere in the village. They have no value.

WORDS to KNOW

LEGAL TENDER: When a government makes one type of money the official currency of that country, this is called legal tender. The legal tender in the United States is the dollar.

TRY THIS

Ready, Set, Trade!
Get a bunch of shells, Legos, or paper clips. Work with a friend and see if you can set up your own system of money. You might decide that one shell is worth one pencil or that two small Legos are worth a stick of gum. Practice using your new currency to buy things from each and see how it works out. What problems do you have?

Metal Money—Coins

Precious metals such as gold and silver came to be widely accepted as valuable. It wasn't long before people found a way to make it into money!

Metal money has several advantages over the other forms of money discussed so far:

- The metals used are scarce. This makes them valuable.
- It is portable—think about how much easier it is to carry several pieces of gold in your pocket than it is to carry baskets of barley!
- Its value is accepted in many countries.
- It is malleable (able to be shaped) and can be divided into little pieces for smaller payments.
- It's beautiful!

Little bean-like lumps of electrum, a gold-silver mixture found in the riverbeds of Lydia (an ancient country in the area that is now Turkey), were the first coins that we know of. Around 630 B.C., the king of Lydia had the lumps stamped with a design of the head of a lion, and coins began to be exchanged for goods in Lydia's markets. The Lydians' coins were so well suited as money that the Greeks and the Romans took to minting (making) coins of their own.

Weighed Down

Metal money was originally traded in lumps, rods, or bars. Its value was in its weight. A bigger (heavier) lump was worth more than a small one. Each time a trade was made, the gold or silver had to be weighed to determine its exact value. As you can imagine, merchants got tired of doing all that weighing! The solution came when merchants began to mark the weight directly on the lump itself.

The EVERYTHING KIDS' Money Book

No Cheaters

In the early days of coins, with gold and silver being such soft metals, a dishonest person was able shave off small pieces of the edge of a coin. This was called "clipping." After a while the cheater would have a collection of clipped pieces large enough to be melted down and sold. If you look at today's quarter, you will notice ridges around the edge. The ridges are known as reeding or milling. Ridges prevented the clipping of coins. If someone tried to clip off a piece of a reeded edge it would be noticed!

So, now the world had coins, and they worked well, but they were inconvenient for making big payments. Imagine having to carry large amounts of coins over great distances. You would need pack animals and you would be an easy target for thieves. Once again, there needed to be a change in currency—paper money.

Fun Fact

Money on Skins

Around 86 B.C., Emperor Wu of China used one-foot squares of white deerskin for money. These squares were decorated around the edges with designs of plants. The emperor decided that each skin would be equal to 400,000 copper coins. This was the beginning of paper money.

$

ISLAND HOPPING

This trader wants to find some more shells. Can you help her get through the island maze to the beach where the shells

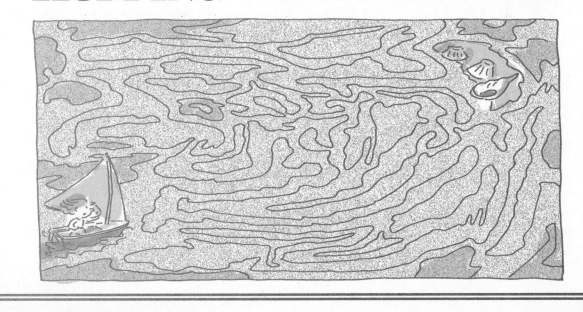

Paper Money

The Chinese are given credit for inventing paper money more than 1,000 years ago. It was not like the bills of today, it was more like today's checks. Merchants put heavy copper coins called cash in the government treasury and were given "certificates of indebtedness" in exchange. Like our modern-day checks, these pieces of paper represented the money that was waiting in the treasury. This check-like money was known as *fei-ch'ien*, or "flying money." Flying, perhaps, because unlike copper, it did not weigh the merchant down!

The Chinese had discovered how to make paper many hundreds of years before the first paper mill in Europe opened in 1189. The Europeans did not rush right out and start making paper money. Improvements in presses used for minting coins made it more convenient for people to continue using metal money. There was little reason to investigate the use of paper money. When you have precious silver or gold in your pocket, why replace it with flimsy paper that can be torn or destroyed?

By the 1600s, though, so much gold and silver was circulating in Europe that people found it was easier to leave their money with someone else for safekeeping. Goldsmiths issued notes that said how much gold had been left with them. These notes were written on paper.

MONEY IS MOBILE

The whole point of money is for it to transfer from person to person. Here's an example of how quickly money can move around:

- You earn $5 walking the neighbor's dog on Monday.
- You spend it at the bookstore that afternoon to buy your mom a birthday present.
- The bookstore clerk gives your $5 bill to the customer behind you in line as change.
- She uses the $5 bill at the movies that night to pay for her popcorn.

- The movie theater deposits the $5 in the bank Tuesday morning.
- A person goes to the bank to withdraw money and gets the $5 bill.
- He leaves that afternoon on vacation to another state and uses the $5 when he gets there to buy a Popsicle.

The money has gone from your hand to another state in two days. Money travels quickly and can move all across the country and even to foreign countries. Money can move slowly as well. If you drop a penny down a sewer grate, it could stay down there for 20 years before it is found. A person could keep a coin in a coin collection his whole life. A dollar bill could stay in a wallet for years without being spent. If you've unexpectedly found a coin in your pocket, you know how easy it is for money to get lost or forgotten.

U.S. dollars usually last about 21 months in circulation. Currently there are 4 billion one dollar bills in use. That's a lot of dough! Dollar bills are made to be used over and over and can be folded approximately 4,000 times before they rip and become unusable.

Money Around the World

Every country in the world has its own money. The only exception is in the European Union (EU). The EU is a group of countries that have formed an alliance or partnership. Most EU countries agreed to stop using their country's own currency and instead use the Euro, currency that is accepted in all EU countries. Belgium, Germany, Spain, France, Ireland, Italy, Luxembourg, the Netherlands, Austria, Portugal, Finland, and Greece agreed to do this. Sweden, Denmark, and the United Kingdom accept the Euro, but still use their own currency. The Euro was designed to increase trade between the EU countries and make it easier for people to move between these countries.

Dollars & Sense

What Money Can't Buy
Although money buys a lot of things, there are lots it can never buy. For example, have you ever been able to buy a real friend? Would money be able to cure you if you were very sick? Absolutely not. Money is very important in our world, but it can't always make you happy.

Where's George?

Ever wonder where your dollar bills have been? Go to *www.wheresgeorge.com* and find out! You can type in the bill's serial number and find out where it has been used and how. Ask a parent to help you set up an account so you can track your bills after you spend them.

Fun Fact

Wampum Was It

Wampum was a Native American currency made from beautifully strung beads made of shells. Purple wampum was the most valuable because purple shells were very rare. In 1641, Massachusetts made wampum legal tender for small transactions, such as the purchase of a bowl. The exchange rate was set as three purple beads or six white beads for one penny.

Money Names Across the World

Country	Type of Money
Australia	Dollar
Brazil	Real
China	Yuan
Czech Republic	Koruna
Denmark	Krone
Ethiopia	Birr
Ghana	Cedi
Haiti	Gourde
India	Rupee
Israel	Shekel
Japan	Yen
Jordan	Dinar
Laos	Kip
Malaysia	Ringgit
Mexico	Peso
Mongolia	Tugrik
Peru	Nuevo Sol
Poland	Zloty
Russia	Ruble
Saudi Arabia	Riyal
South Korea	Won
Sweden	Krona
Thailand	Baht
United Kingdom	Pound
Venezuela	Bolivar
Zambia	Kwacha

What to Do with Money: Earn, Save, Spend

Money is totally awesome because there are so many things you can do with it. To get money you've first got to earn it. You can do this by working, investing, or getting gifts. Having someone hand you some cash is a terrific feeling, but deciding what to do with it can be challenging.

Once you've got money, you have lots of choices about how to use it. You can save your money and watch it slowly grow in a piggy bank or in a real bank. You might find it's fun to see how much you can save. Keep adding to your stash to see how much you can get. You might also enjoy looking at the actual bills and coins and collecting them.

Money is also for spending. Think of all the things you can buy with money—toys, food, music, books, movies, games, skateboards, and more. Our economy is based on people spending money.

Government Stash: The U.S. Bank

It's difficult for us to imagine, but in the early years of the United States, the government was not in charge of issuing paper money. Instead, individual banks issued paper money. The bills were promises that the bank would exchange the paper notes for their value in gold or silver coins.

Each colony printed its own money and some even had to rely on French money because it was more easily available and more

How to Make Money

You can make your own play money. Draw pretend bills, cut them out, and begin to do some trading. See how much you can save or spend. The nice difference between this game and real life is you can always draw more money!

people accepted it as payment. Having so many kinds of money made it hard to trade. Imagine if you went to the store to buy hockey cards and you had dollars but one store only took Mexican pesos and another Japanese yen. It would make it hard to buy anything. The newly formed U.S. government attempted to put an end to some of these confusing money situations that made life in the colonies difficult. In 1791, shortly after the adoption of the Constitution, Congress chartered the first Bank of the United States and gave it the power to issue bank notes.

The banking business was rocky in the first half of the nineteenth century. In the 1810s, Congress almost didn't renew the charter of the first Bank of the United States! Congress only rechartered the bank because it wasn't able to borrow enough money from state banks to pay for the War of 1812! The next time the bank's charter came up for renewal in the 1830s, Congress did not renew it. Once again the United States was in a big mess money-wise!

Your Friend, The Fed

In 1913, Congress set up the Federal Reserve System, also known as the Fed. Congress gave the Fed the power "to coin money, and to regulate the value thereof," or to print money and decide how much it's worth.

The Fed acts as the central bank of the United States. Its activities are separate from the U.S. Treasury (which creates and distributes money). The Fed is the bank that the federal government uses to pay its bills. For example, if your grandparents get Social Security checks from the government each month, these checks represent money in the Treasury account at the Federal Reserve Bank.

What else does the Fed do? Lots!

- The Fed distributes newly minted and printed currency to banks.
- Federal Reserve banks check the condition of money they receive. If bills are worn and torn, the Fed destroys them by shredding. If counterfeit (fake) bills are found, they are stamped "counterfeit" and sent to the U.S. Secret Service for investigation. Coins that are badly worn or bent are removed from circulation (general use), and so are foreign coins. The Fed advises the U.S. Treasury when more currency needs to be minted or printed to replace damaged currency.
- The Fed makes up rules for banks to follow.
- Every day millions of payments, both by check and through electronic funds transfer, are handled by Federal Reserve Banks. Non-Federal Reserve banks can buy check clearing services (where a company checks with a bank to make sure there is enough money to cover a check that has been written from the Fed rather than going to other check clearing houses (businesses that clear checks).
- If a bank needs money and it cannot borrow from another non-Federal-Reserve bank, then the Fed can give the bank a loan.

There are twelve main Federal Reserve Banks. Each of them is in charge of a certain area of the country, and they all have smaller branches throughout their territory. The main banks are in Atlanta, Boston, Cleveland, Dallas, Kansas City, Minneapolis, New York, Philadelphia, Richmond, St. Louis, and San Francisco. Which bank is closest to you?

Dollars & Sense

Dirty Money
Because money is transferred from person to person so often, it picks up germs. One study found that 42% of dollar bills are bacteria carriers. After you count your money or spend a lot of time handling cash (like at a lemonade stand) it's a good idea to wash your hands!

SPACE TRADE

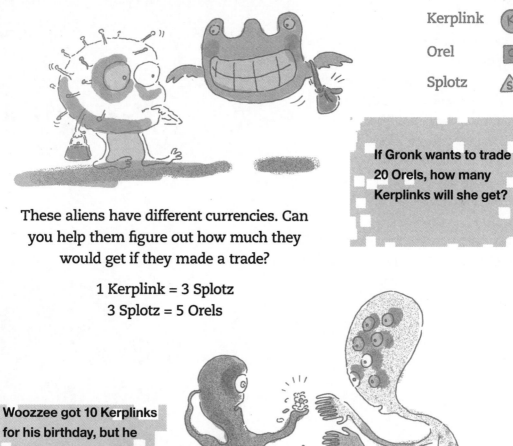

Kerplink ⓚ

Orel ▣

Splotz △ⓢ

These aliens have different currencies. Can you help them figure out how much they would get if they made a trade?

1 Kerplink = 3 Splotz
3 Splotz = 5 Orels

If Gronk wants to trade 20 Orels, how many Kerplinks will she get?

Woozzee got 10 Kerplinks for his birthday, but he wants to buy something at Leefoo's store. She only uses Splotz. How many Splotz will he get if he makes a trade?

Alien Money If aliens had money, what do you think it would look like? Get some paper and crayons and make some for yourself. That way if an alien lands you can buy his spaceship!

Fun Fact

Coin Protectors

During the Salem witch trials in 1692, superstitious people wore bent coins as a way to protect themselves from witches. Many of the coins from this era that still exist show signs of having been bent!

$

OUR COUNTRY IN COINS

There was a shortage of coins in the American colonies during the seventeenth and eighteenth centuries. Colonists had to depend on non-coin types of money to conduct business. A number of colonies used wampum, tobacco, or other commodity money.

Why wasn't there enough currency? One reason is that money was sent back to England to buy things that weren't available in America. The goods were shipped to the colonies, but the money stayed in England. Another reason is that the British government did not want to send its coins to the colonies. It was a form of control.

Mixed-Up Money

Since ships came to the Americas from countries such as Portugal and France, coins other than English ones made their way into the economy. Due to trade with the Spanish West Indies, eight-reales silver coins became popular. These Spanish milled dollars were also known as "pieces of eight" because they could be cut into eight parts, or "bits." Each bit was worth twelve and a half cents.

Some of the Spanish dollars were minted in Mexico City from the rich supply of Mexican silver. The dollars were readily available to the colonists and were accepted for financial transactions. Another Spanish coin, the gold doubloon, was equal in value to sixteen of the silver dollar coins.

Making Money

But still, there was not enough coinage to go around, and the colonies began to mint coins in smaller denominations to meet the demand for coins. In 1652, John Hull of the Massachusetts Bay Colony started a mint that produced very simple coins. The coins were stamped with NE for New England on one side and the denomination on the other. The simplicity of the coin led to trouble—it was easy to counterfeit and easy to clip.

From 1653 to 1674, Hull's mint produced redesigned coins that had a willow, oak, or pine tree on the obverse (front of the coin). On the reverse (back of the coin), the coins had the date and III, VI, or XII (the Roman numerals for 3 = threepence, 6 = sixpence, and 12 = shilling). Hull's coins are usually referred to as New England pine tree coins.

Coin Confusion

Other colonies began to mint coins too. There were different coins in each of the colonies. The values placed on the coins in each region also differed and often led to confusion. In his autobiography, Benjamin Franklin tells of going to a bakery in Philadelphia after his move from Boston:

> Then I asked for a three-penny loaf, and was told they had none such. So not considering or knowing the difference of money, and the greater cheapness nor the names of his bread, I made him give me three-penny worth of any sort. He gave me, accordingly, three great puffy rolls. I was surpriz'd at the quantity, but took it, and, having no room in my pockets, walk'd off with a roll under each arm, and eating the other.

Imagine how confusing things got by the end of the eighteenth century when the British had been defeated and each of the states was minting its own coins! Take, for example, Connecticut. During the years from 1785 to 1788, more than 300 different copper coins were made! Why so many? The state authorized private citizens to mint the coins for the state. Each mint developed its own design!

Individual states did not always find it easy to mint their own coins. In 1787 and 1788, when the state of

Making Cents

It now costs 1.4 cents to make each penny and there is a movement to do away with the penny (*www.retirethepenny.org*). What changes would have to happen if we did eliminate the penny? How would this affect you? Do you think it's a good idea or a bad idea?

Massachusetts began to make copper cents and half cents, it found that it cost two cents to make each cent, and one cent to make a half cent! Massachusetts only operated its mint for a short time.

U.S. Coins Are Born

By 1787 it was time for the United States to think about producing a national coin. James Jarvis was given a contract by Congress to produce 300 tons of copper coins. Jarvis minted a coin known as the "Fugio" cent. The Fugio cent is the first official coin of the United States.

The cent had a sundial on the obverse and the Latin word *fugio*, meaning "I fly." This was a reference to the old saying, "time flies." Also on the front is the legend "mind your business." Mind your business refers to the citizens of the United States having to build up their businesses to make for a stronger country. It had nothing to do with nosiness!

The reverse of the Fugio cent had a chain with thirteen links representing the thirteen states, and the motto "we are one."

Fresh Mint

Congress adopted the U.S. Constitution in 1791. One of Congress's first acts was to create the U.S. Mint. Construction of the building began shortly thereafter in Philadelphia. The Coinage Act of April 1792 set up a system of coin denominations. Ten coins were chosen:

- a $10 gold eagle
- a $5 gold half-eagle
- a $2.50 gold quarter-eagle
- a silver dollar
- a silver half-dollar
- a silver quarter-dollar

The EVERYTHING KIDS' Money Book

- a silver-disme (*disme* is another word for a dime)
- a silver half-disme
- a copper cent
- a copper half-cent piece

It also allowed for the coins to be minted with the legend, "United States of America."

Before the construction of the mint building in Philadelphia was finished, 1,500 coins were produced by a private mint. It is believed that George Washington and his wife, Martha, donated some of their silver utensils for the minting. These first official coins were half-dismes dated 1792.

The following year, 1793, the Philadelphia mint started producing larger numbers of coins for general circulation. The first to be issued were the copper cent and half-cent pieces. It wasn't until 1796 that all the denominations were being made.

Branching Out

As the border of the United States expanded, the mint in Philadelphia was unable to keep up with the demand for coins. The first branch mints were set up in 1838. Today there are branches in San Francisco, California; Denver, Colorado; and West Point, New York.

The branches put mint marks on the coins they produced—an "S" for San Francisco, a "D" for Denver, and a "W" for West Point. Philadelphia has a mint mark "P," but it does not appear on cents or on coins made before 1980, with two exceptions—the 1942–45 nickels and the 1979 Susan B. Anthony dollars.

Money Trouble

Now that the United States had its own coins, all its money problems were over, right? Wrong! Unfortunately, not enough currency remained in circulation. It seems that the many silver and gold coins were sent to other

Fun Fact

Tea for Cents

There are several stories about where the 300 tons of copper used in the Fugio cents came from. One is that the copper was left over from the metal bands that held together powder kegs used in the Revolutionary War. Another is that many U.S. citizens, including Ben Franklin, donated their copper teapots!

Coin Hunt

There are three valuable coins in here, but they're hard to spot. Can you find the coins where the man has an eye patch, a flower on his jacket, and a beard?

countries by metals speculators (people who traded and tried to make money from metal). The coins were melted down and sold. The value of the metals in foreign countries was more than the value of the coins in the United States.

In 1852, Congress passed a law that allowed for coins to be minted with a metal value less than the face value of the coin. In other words, a silver dollar no longer had a dollar's worth of silver in it. The content of all the U.S. silver coins was reduced by 7 percent. A silver dollar after 1852 had a silver content of 93 percent, so it was no longer profitable for metals speculators to ship the coins overseas.

Even though the United States had its own national coins during the period from the late 1790s until the 1850s, foreign coins continued to be used in the United States! In 1857 Congress finally outlawed the use of foreign currency as legal tender.

Coins Today

Today the following coin denominations are being circulated in the United States:

- one cent (penny)
- five-cent piece (nickel)
- ten-cent piece (dime)
- twenty-five cent piece (quarter)
- fifty-cent piece (half-dollar)
- dollar

There are no coins that are made of one metal—all U.S. coins contain alloys (mixtures of two or more metals).

The Penny

The half-cent copper piece was minted only until 1857. The coin we know as the penny is officially called a cent. *Penny* is a popular carryover from the days of the British copper pennies. The cents produced from 1793 to 1857 are known as large cents. That coin was even larger than our present-day quarter! The very first cent issued had an image of Liberty with wild flowing hair on the obverse. On the reverse was a chain with 13 links surrounded by the words "United States of Ameri." It was later redesigned so the full word *America* would fit at the end.

The large cent was replaced by a cent piece the same size as the one we know today. Until 1909, the head of an Indian in a headdress was on the obverse. A wreath decorated the reverse. In 1909, for the 100th anniversary of Abraham Lincoln's birth, the coin was redesigned with the head of Lincoln on the obverse and two ears of wheat on the reverse. In honor of the 150th anniversary of Lincoln's birth in 1959, the wheat on the reverse of the cent was replaced by the Lincoln Memorial.

The Nickel

The half-dime was only minted until 1873 and it was even smaller than today's dime. In 1866, the nickel five-cent piece was introduced. It was the first non-silver five-cent coin and was made of 25 percent nickel and 75 percent copper. Its common name, *nickel*, came from its nickel content. The first nickel had a shield design on the obverse. In 1883 the shield design was replaced with a Liberty head.

The next big change in the nickel took place in 1913 with the introduction of the Indian head (obverse) or Buffalo (reverse) type nickels. The Jefferson nickel—which featured an obverse view of Jefferson himself and a reverse view of Monticello, his home—was introduced in 1938. The nickel was changed yet again in 2004. Two different reverse sides were created to commemorate

Dollars & Sense

Wish Another Way

People often make a wish and throw a coin into a fountain or pool of water. This can be dangerous to the animals that live in the water or use it for drinking. Current U.S. pennies are mainly made of zinc. The zinc is poisonous. If you must throw something, use a pebble instead.

Fun Fact

Bison Posing as Buffalo

The animal on the Buffalo nickel was modeled after an American bison named Black Diamond. Black Diamond did not roam the plains out west. He lived at New York's Central Park Zoo!

the Lewis and Clark expedition. One coin shows the design from a peace medal, with a European American and Native American shaking hands. The other shows the keelboat Lewis and Clark used for their expedition.

In 2005 yet another new design was introduced with a bigger silhouette of Jefferson on the obverse and two reverse designs. One is an American bison and the other shows the Pacific Ocean, which Lewis and Clark eventually reached. In 2006 the coin was updated again to show Jefferson's face from the front, with his home, Monticello, on the reverse.

The Dime

The dime has been continuously minted since 1796. For its first ninety-six years an obviously feminine Liberty appeared on the obverse. In 1892, with a series of coins known as "Barber" type (named for the designer of the coin), Liberty's appearance changed; she took on a more masculine look. Then, in 1916, Liberty appeared with a winged helmet on her head! It was thought that this image was of the Greek god Mercury and so the dimes from 1916 to 1945 are known as Mercury dimes. Franklin Roosevelt dimes were introduced in 1946, shortly after President Roosevelt's death, and are the current dime today.

The Quarter

Quarter-dollars, or quarters as we know them, have gone through many changes since 1796. There have been more than thirteen types, and, except for the last type, the Washington head, all have had Liberty on the obverse and an eagle on the reverse. The Washington head was introduced in 1932 to honor George Washington's 200th birthday!

For 1976, in celebration of the U.S. bicentennial, a temporary reverse design appeared—a colonial drummer. The obverse also carried the double date, 1776–

1976. The half-dollar and the Eisenhower dollar coins also went through a bicentennial redesign.

An exciting change to the quarter began taking place in 1999. In 1999 five new quarters were introduced as part of the Fifty State Program, a program designed to celebrate all U.S. states. The obverse of the coin stays the same, but each state gets a chance to design the reverse to highlight what makes it special. The new coins have been introduced five per year. The coins are released in the same order that the states signed the Constitution or entered the Union.

The design of these new coins was a cooperative effort. State governors submitted designs to the U.S. Mint and several other groups. The secretary of the Treasury approved the final design. There were several limits placed on the design. The coins may not contain a traditional bust (head and shoulders) of any living or dead person. No state flags or seals were to appear. It was suggested that landmarks, state symbols, historical buildings, and outlines of the state were all appropriate.

Delaware, having been the first to sign the Constitution, had the honor of being represented in the first release. The design chosen for Delaware's coin is of a colonial rider on a horse. The rider is Caesar Rodney. The image represents his ride to Independence Hall in Philadelphia to sign the Constitution in 1776.

Half-Dollar

The half-dollar, also known as the fifty-cent piece, has been made nearly every year since 1794. Quick, do you know whose image appears on the latest half-dollar issue? If you said John F. Kennedy, you are correct. Half-dollars are not used as frequently as other coins.

Dollar Coins

Dollar coins were originally issued in silver, but in the late 1800s a gold dollar was also produced. The last

PENNY FOR YOUR THOUGHTS

Stately Designs
What does your state's design look like? Would you have chosen that design or would you have wanted to celebrate a different aspect of your state's history or geography?

MONEY MEMORIES

In 1986 commemorative coins were made to celebrate the 100th anniversary of the Statue of Liberty. The statue was presented to the United States from France as a gift in 1886. It looks like the statue on the right is a fake. Can you spot the seven differences?

Here's a fun activity: Why not commemorate somebody you think should be remembered or celebrated? You could draw your own coin or just a big blue ribbon with her name on it!

The EVERYTHING KIDS· Money Book

dollar that was 90 percent silver appeared in 1935. In 1971, the Dwight D. Eisenhower silver dollar was introduced. This last of the silver dollars was only 40 percent silver! It was not produced after 1974.

Susan B. Anthony Coin

The Susan B. Anthony dollar was first minted in 1979. People complained about its size when it was first released. It was only slightly larger than the quarter, and it also had reeded edging. People thought the similarity to the quarter would be confusing and result in errors being made in making change, or that the coin would jam in vending machines.

The public, for the most part, refused to use the new coin, and production ceased in 1981. Supplies of the coins were kept warehoused in vaults until 1993 when the U.S. Postal Service installed new vending machines in post offices. The machines for making change to purchase stamps gave the Susan B. Anthony coin as change for $5 bills. The Susan B. came back to life!

Today, nineteen of the top twenty-five transit systems around the country, including New York and Chicago, use the dollar coin in vending machines. The supplies in the government vaults dwindled until 1999 when there was some question as to whether the U.S. Mint needed to produce new Susan B. Anthony dollars to keep up with the demand!

The advantages of a dollar coin were becoming more obvious. A coin will last twenty-five to thirty years. A paper dollar lasts only one and a half years! Even with the higher manufacturing costs of the coin— eight cents as compared with four cents for the paper— the greater life of the coin makes it an economically sound choice. The U.S. Government Accounting Office estimates that the government could save $395 million a year by making dollar coins instead of paper one dollar bills.

TRY THIS

Coin Toss

Ever wonder what would happen if you flipped a coin 100 times? Probability says you will usually end up flipping 50 heads and 50 tails. Start a log and start flipping to see what happens!

Sacagawea Dollar

The Sacagawea coin was released in 2000. The obverse has the image of Sacagawea—the Native American Shoshone woman who guided the Lewis and Clark expedition to the Pacific Ocean in 1804–1806—looking over her shoulder and carrying her young son, Jean Baptiste. On the reverse is a flying eagle surrounded by seventeen stars, representing the number of states at the time of the Lewis and Clark expedition.

Presidential and First Spouse Dollars

In 2007, the Presidential and First Spouse $1 coin program was introduced. The program will run for ten years. Each presidential coin honors a U.S. president who has been dead at least two years. They are created in the order in which the presidents served in office. These dollars will circulate alongside the Sacagawea dollar.

For each president, the front of the coin will feature the president's portrait, name, and the years the president's term began and ended. An image of the Statue of Liberty will appear on the back of each coin.

Several features have been moved to the edge of the coin, a first in U.S. coins. The phrases "E Pluribus Unum" and "In God We Trust," the year of the minting, and the mint mark all appear on the edge of this coin.

The obverse of each first spouse coin features a portrait of the woman each president was married to while he was in office. The reverse shows each first lady doing what she was known for. However, Thomas Jefferson's wife, Martha, died long before he became president. This happened to several other presidents as well. In these cases, the coin celebrates the president's term in office. The obverse of the coin is an image of Liberty, and the reverse illustrates a key moment in the president's life. Andrew Jackson, whose wife died shortly after he was elected, is shown on horseback. His old war nickname, Old Hickory, is etched into the space beside him.

Melted Metal

The process to create a new coin is complex. A design must be created and approved by the secretary of the Treasury. Then a coin can be made! To do that, a die must be produced.

A sculptor-engraver at the U.S. Mint makes a model out of Plasticene, a non-hardening type of modeling clay. The model is three to twelve times larger than the finished coin. Then, several plaster of Paris models are made, and the final model is called a galvano. With each step the models are adjusted so that all the detail in the design sketches is reproduced. The final model must be approved by Mint officials before the process continues to the next step.

The galvano is put on a machine called a transfer engraving machine. The machine cuts the design in a steel blank that is the same size as the finished coin, producing a hub. A hub is used to make the dies that strike the coins. There is one die for the obverse and one for the reverse.

The Birth of a Coin

Now the actual coins can be made. First, large sheets of metal called coin strip are fed into presses that cut out blanks, also known as planchets. The planchets are softened in a furnace in a process called annealing. Then they are washed and dried and put on a riddler to screen out coins of the wrong shape and size.

Next, the planchets are put through the upsetting machine. The upsetting machine forms the raised edges of the coins, and the edges are hardened during this stage. The hardening is a necessary step. If the edges aren't hard when the coin is struck, some of the metal could squirt out!

TRY THIS

Shine Up Your Pennies
Place ¼ cup of vinegar and 1 teaspoon of salt in a small bowl. Take your dirty pennies (NOT any that are collectible or valuable) and soak them in the solution for five minutes. Rinse and let them air dry. They will be bright and shiny! For even more fun, save the vinegar solution when you're done and soak a nail or screw in it for an hour. It will turn copper! Copper ions left in the water attach to the iron in the nail.

It can be tempting to want to keep the coins in your collection looking shiny and new, but cleaning a coin can actually reduce its value. Even using a soft cloth to wipe a coin can cause small scratches. If your coin has dirt or something sticky on it, your best bet is to soak it in olive oil for a few days, rinse it, and then let it air dry.

After the planchets have been upset, they go to the coining presses where the two dies are already set up. The planchet is struck only once to make a coin. Dimes, quarters, and half-dollars get reeded edges at the same time that they are struck. The finished coins are inspected, counted, bagged, and then shipped off to Federal Reserve Banks for distribution.

DECODING COINS

There are several things that are required by law to be on all U.S. coins:

- "LIBERTY"
- An image of Liberty, usually a female form
- "In God We Trust"
- The date
- The denomination
- "United States of America"
- "E Pluribus Unum" (Latin for "out of many, one," meaning many states come together to make our one country)
- An eagle on coins larger than a dime

Exceptions are made, though, such as with the state quarter designs.

COIN COLLECTING FUN

Are all coins collectible? Absolutely! If you find them beautiful or interesting, then that's reason enough for you to collect them. But only the valuable ones can be bought and sold for investment purposes.

What gives collectible coins their value? Two things: rarity and condition. If only a few examples of a particular coin are known to exist, then their rarity makes them valuable.

Condition is the shape the coin is in. The best condition is known as "mint" condition; the coin is as good as the day it came from the mint. The more worn a coin becomes, the poorer its condition and the less it is worth. However, a coin in poor condition could still have value if it is rare!

Determining Value

How do you find the value of a coin?

- Check a price guide such as the *Guide to U.S. Coins, Prices and Value Trends* by the editors of *Coin World*.
- Read coin collecting magazines such as *Coin Prices* and *Coins*.
- Talk to coin dealers and numismatists (coin experts).
- Go to coin shows and join coin collectors' organizations.
- Visit coin collecting websites.

COPPER COUNTERFEIT

At one point there were so many different coins being made that it was difficult to tell the real from the fake. Can you see which coin follows the first two?

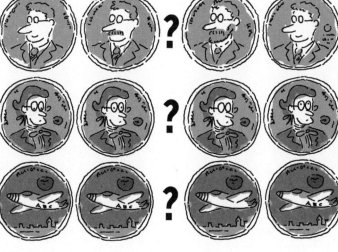

You may be surprised to find that some of the coins you have around the house are more valuable than you expected! You might also be surprised to find out that some very old coins you thought were valuable are not worth much at all!

Finding Coins

Where can you find collectible coins? You can find them at coin shops and coin shows, through mail order, or online. The U.S. Mint has special proof sets (specially designed coins with frosted, sculpted details) of coins that you can buy directly from the Mint.

Dump out your piggy bank and sort through those coins. You can also check with your parents and grandparents to see if they have any old coins. If they do, ask if you could research them. Look them up in price guides and find out their history. If you're lucky, you'll find something of value.

What kinds of coins should you collect? The best idea is to collect the things that interest you. It could be silver dollars, minting errors, or perhaps you'd like to collect one dime from every year they were minted. If you'd like to collect foreign coins, you could specialize in coins that have ships on them, or ones that have trees. Or you might be excited at the thought of creating a complete collection of presidential dollar coins or state quarters. The choice is yours.

Slowly But Surely

Investing in coins takes time and patience. It may take you years to collect a dime from every year, but think of all the fun you'll have doing it. It's the thrill of the hunt! In 1804 there were only 8,265 dimes minted. How many of these do you think survived over the 200 years since they were minted? Imagine adding one of the 1804s to your collection. You may have to wait until you grow up and get a job before you can afford one!

On August 30, 1999, a silver dollar minted in 1804, one of only fifteen known pieces, went on the auction block and sold for a record-breaking $4.14 million! Another of these 1804 dollars had sold in 1997 for $1.815 million. Imagine if you bought a silver dollar at $1.815 million and turned around and sold it two years later for $4.14 million! You would have more than doubled your investment!

But coin collecting doesn't have to be expensive in order to be fun. If you collect all fifty state quarters, it will only cost you $12.50.

Dollars & Sense

Protect Your Coins

If you have a coin collection, it's fun to sort through the coins, touch them, and look at them. If you're serious about it, though, your valuable coins should not be touched. Keep them in protective plastic sleeves. Scratches and damage will decrease their value.

BILL BONANZA

As you read in Chapter 1, North America's first paper money was actually playing cards that the governor of New France wrote on as a promise to pay his soldiers. We've come a long way since then!

Paper Notes

The Canadian notes did not work as well as planned, but it didn't stop the colonists in Massachusetts Bay Colony from following Canada's lead. The Colony issued paper notes in 1690 to pay soldiers for their service against Canada in King William's War. The trouble with these "Old Charter" bills was that they were not legal tender. The only thing they could be used for was paying taxes!

Throughout the colonies coins were scarce and expensive to produce. A reasonable alternative was paper notes. Notes were printed in denominations as small as three pence! Most of the notes were issued in denominations based on the British monetary system, but some notes had values in Spanish dollars. Each colony produced its own notes, and like coinage in early America, paper money values varied.

Continentals

During the Revolutionary War, the colonists needed to raise money to pay for their fight against the British. The Continental Congress issued paper money called "Continentals," with values in dollars, not British pounds!

Unfortunately, the colonies had nothing to back up their money. The Continental Congress had planned on collecting taxes so there would be enough money to pay the notes, but the plan fell through (it only had the power to ask for taxes and could not force them to be paid). To add to the problem, the notes were easily counterfeited. All in all, the Continental was a failure. "Not worth a Continental" is a phrase that was once common in the United States and it meant something of little or no value. That sums up the fate of the Continental!

Bank Notes Begin

States chartered many banks, but they did a poor job of regulating them. Almost anyone could start up a bank and print bank notes. Bank notes were printed without enough actual money to back them up. By 1836 there were about 1,600 banks and more than 30,000 different bank notes!

Banks failed frequently, especially in the Panic of 1837, when President Jackson's failure to renew the charter of the Second Bank of the United States triggered an economic crisis. People went to the banks looking to exchange paper notes for gold and silver. Those banks that did not have the metal to back the notes went bankrupt. Today, paper money collectors call the bank notes from this time "broken bank notes" because most of the banks went broke!

National Bills

By the start of the Civil War the banking system was in chaos. Coins were once again in short supply and the United States had no reliable system by which it could pay for the war. Congress gave the U.S. Treasury the authority to issue demand notes, or notes that would allow the holder of the note to demand payment. These notes took the place of money and were like a written promise to pay.

The demand notes issued in 1861 were replaced the following year by United States Notes. The United States Notes, also known as legal tender notes, were commonly referred to as greenbacks. National Bank Notes were formally allowed by Congress through the National Banking Act of 1863. They continued to be circulated until the 1920s. The stock market crash of 1929

TRY THIS

Magic Dollar Bill
Fold the short side of a dollar bill one third over. Attach a paper clip. Fold the other end one third over and attach a paper clip there as well. Slowly pull the edges of the bill apart. When it is fully straightened out, the paper clips will fly into the air, attached to each other!

Dollars & Sense

Dollar Don'ts
It's a crime to make color copies of U.S. bills. If you ever want to copy a bill, you may only do so in black and white. You may not make a copy the same size, either. You must blow the copy up to be 150 percent larger than an actual bill.

brought about the end of the bank note in the United States.

In 1913, with the establishment of the Federal Reserve System, the Fed starting issuing paper money (see Chapter 1 for more on the Fed). Federal Reserve Notes make up 99 percent of all paper money in circulation in the United States today.

Go for the Gold

Two other types of notes need to be mentioned—gold certificates and silver certificates. Gold certificates, starting in 1865, could be exchanged for gold coins or bullion. They were in circulation until 1933. Silver certificates could be exchanged for silver dollars starting in 1878. These bills remained in circulation until 1963, although they could not be exchanged for silver dollars after 1934.

COUNT ON IT: PAPER MONEY TODAY

Today, all U.S. bills are printed by the Bureau of Engraving and Printing, which is part of the U.S. Treasury. In 1929, big changes were made in U.S. paper notes. The size was reduced by 25 percent to make the bills easier to handle and the design was standardized for all the denominations. Very few changes were made until 1994, when paper currency was redesigned to add anti-counterfeiting and other features. These newly designed bills are being added over a period of years. The first to be introduced was the $100 note in 1996.

There are seven denominations of paper money currently being produced: $1, $2, $5, $10, $20, $50, and $100. At one time there were also $500, $1,000, $5,000, and $10,000 bills, but these haven't been printed since 1946. The largest U.S. bill ever was the $100,000, and only 42,000 were produced, all in 1934. The $100,000 bill was

BILLFOLD

A billfold is the same as a wallet—it's somewhere to put your money. All the words on the left start with B-I-L-L and all the words on the right end with F-O-L-D. Can you figure them out?

Advertisements go on a BILL_____.

1,000 million equals 1 BILL___.

This game has pockets: BILL_____.

In the wind a sail can BILL__.

A raised platform is a ____FOLD.

To open a towel you __FOLD.

Twice as big or twice as many is ___FOLD.

To tie around someone's eyes so they can't see is to _____FOLD.

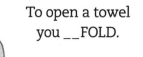

BILL_____
BILL_____
BILL_____
BILL____

_ _ FOLD
_ _ _ FOLD
_ _ _ FOLD
_ _ _ FOLD

Fold It Up
It is believed billfolds were created in the 1600s, soon after the introduction of paper currency.
Before that money consisted of coins.

TRY THIS

Design Your Own Dollar!

Imagine you have your own country and need to create money. Cut out a piece of paper about the size of a dollar bill. Use markers, crayons, or paints and create your own bill. Don't forget to include your country's name, the amount of each bill, and maybe some special identifying features. What will you call your form of money? Come up with a cool name!

It's Raining Bills

Large amounts of new money are printed each year. Check out the number of bills that are created every year:

- $1 bills: 4.5 billion
- $5 bills: 800 million
- $10 bills: 851 million
- $20 bills: 889 million
- $100 bills: 950 million

Not all denominations are printed every year. The $50 and $2 bills are only printed every few years.

Dead Dollars

The U.S Treasury is in charge of making sure that money in circulation is in good condition. Ever wonder what would happen if a bill you had got ripped or damaged? As long as you have at least half of the bill, you can take it to your bank and exchange it for another bill. The U.S. Treasury will exchange it for the bank. Every year the U.S. Treasury handles approximately 30,000 claims and exchanges mutilated currency valued at more than $30 million.

Damaged paper bills are shredded and recycled. The U.S. Treasury shreds and recycles 715 million bills each year. Can you imagine having a job where you destroy money every day?

SECRETS IN YOUR WALLET! HOW TO READ A DOLLAR BILL

Take a look at both sides of a one dollar bill to see what all the words, numbers, and pictures mean.

On the Front

1. **"Federal Reserve Note."** About 99 percent of all currency now in circulation are Federal Reserve Notes. These notes are printed to meet the demand of the Federal Reserve System.
2. **"The United States of America."** This tells everyone that this paper money is from the United States. It also appears on the back of the bill.
3. **Federal Reserve District Seal.** Each of the twelve Federal Reserve Districts has its own seal.
4. **Serial number.** Each bill has its own serial number. No number is repeated within the same denomination and series. Notice the letter at the beginning. It refers to the Federal Reserve Bank. The letter at the end of the serial number refers to the print run. The first run is "A." In each run, the numbers go from 00000001–99999999. What run was your bill done on? A serial number with a star at the end tells us that the bill is a replacement for one that was destroyed during the printing process. These are referred to as star notes.
5. **"This note is legal tender for all debts, public and private."** The United States has decided that this currency is valid for the payment of all debts within the United States.
6. **Signatures.** There are always two signatures on the bill—one belongs to the treasurer of the United States, and the other belongs to the secretary of the Treasury.
7. **Treasury Department Seal.** The seal is printed in green ink over the denomination printing done in black.

SEAL IT UP

Somebody has been tampering with the great seal. Can you spot the six changes?

Good Luck 13
There are thirteen levels of the pyramid, and it has been left unfinished to show that America is always growing.

8. **Check letter.** The letter is the same in both the upper left and lower right corners.

9. **Denomination.** The denomination is spelled out twice, once on the front on the right side of the bill, once on the back in the middle, and appears as a number in the four corners.

10. **Portrait.** No living person may appear on U.S. currency. Presidents, in this case George Washington, appear on all the denominations currently being printed except for the $10 and $100 bills. Do you know who appears on these? Alexander Hamilton graces the $10, and Benjamin Franklin's portrait is on the $100. And in case you didn't know, the presidents on the other bills are: $2—Thomas Jefferson, $5—Abraham Lincoln; $20—Andrew Jackson; and $50—Ulysses S. Grant.

11. **Series.** Every time a new design is used or a new secretary of the Treasury is appointed by the president and approved by Congress, the series date changes. If a bill has a letter after the date, it means a very minor design change has been made, or a new treasurer has been appointed by the president.

On the Back

1. **Denomination.** The amount is written out six times and written as a number four times.

2. **"In God We Trust."** By law, this motto appears on all U.S. coins and currency.

3. **Plate number.** The plate used to print the back of the bill.

4. **The Great Seal of the United States.** The two sides of the Great Seal are reproduced on the one dollar bill. On its obverse is the American bald eagle. *E Pluribus Unum* means "out of many, one." The olive branch symbolizes peace. The arrows symbolize the fight for liberty, and the cloud and stars above the eagle's head represent God and the light shining in the darkness. On the reverse is a pyramid symbol-

The EVERYTHING KIDS· Money Book

izing strength and, like the pyramids of Egypt, long life. It is unfinished to indicate that the United States continues to be built. The Roman numeral at the base is the number 1776. *Annuit Coeptis* is Latin for "He has smiled on our undertakings," meaning God has favored the United States. The eye represents the eye of God. The other Latin motto, *Novus Ordo Seclorum*, means "a new order of the ages." The new order refers to the new nation. The original Great Seal is made of brass (the one used today is made of steel) and is impressed into important papers to make them legal.

For information about what appears on the other denominations, read Nancy Winslow Parker's book *Money, Money, Money: The Meaning of the Art and Symbols on United States Paper Currency* (HarperCollins Children's Books, 1995). To learn about the artwork on money in other countries, read David Standish's *The Art of Money* (Chronicle Books, 2000).

WHAT'S IT WORTH?

You know that a dollar bill is worth $1, but did you know that the value of that dollar actually changes? Money is valued by looking at what it will buy. If a dollar will buy you a candy bar today, but tomorrow you need two dollars to buy that same candy bar, then the value of the money has changed.

George Washington was paid $25,000 a year to be president. The current president earns about $400,000 a year. The job hasn't changed, but the value of the dollar has. Inflation is what happens when the prices of things go up. Inflation means money will buy less than it did before.

When inflation increases faster than the increase in people's salaries, it means people are able to buy less. Using the previous example, if you had $2 yesterday and

Fun Fact
The Origin of $
The origin of the $ sign is thought to have come from the Mexican or Spanish "Ps" for pesos, or piastres, or pieces of eight. In old manuscripts, the "S" gradually was written over the "P," which looks like the $ sign. Eventually $ was written instead.

could buy two $1 candy bars, but today the price has gone up and your $2 will only pay for one candy bar, you've just been hit with inflation!

The value of money used to be based on the actual value of the bushel of barley or precious metal in the coin you had in your hands. Today, we don't melt down our quarters, so the money we use has come to have a symbolic value.

BIRTH OF A BILL

Ever wonder how dollar bills are made? It's complicated. There are 65 separate steps!

The Bureau of Engraving and Printing prints money on high-speed printers that can print more than 8,000 sheets per hour. They print about 22.5 million bills each day.

When money is printed, printing plates made of soft steel are created to reflect the design that has been approved by the Department of the Treasury. Each plate is made with engravings in it; engravings are cuts in the metal that make up all the words and designs that will be on the bills. The plates are covered with ink and then the surface of each plate is wiped clean. The ink remains in the grooves of the plates.

Special paper is used to print bills. The paper has no wood fiber at all and is made of 75 percent cotton and 25 percent linen. It has tiny blue and red silk threads embedded in it. The paper has been made by Crane and Company, Inc., since 1879. The formula is a secret (shh!), but one thing we know is that it is made out of scraps of denim—the same material your jeans are made from!

When it's time to print the money, the paper is moistened and each sheet is pressed between the specially made plates. The ink is transferred to the paper. The surface of the note feels slightly raised, while the reverse side feels slightly indented. This process is called intaglio printing. The back of the bill is then printed with green ink and allowed to dry for one or two days, then the portrait on the front is printed with black ink. The sheets of bills are then cut in half and inspected. The sheets go through another printer that adds the Federal Reserve and Treasury seals. Finally, they are cut to make individual bills. The bills are bundled up into bricks of 100 bills.

No Cheating!

Counterfeiting is making a copy of a note in an attempt to defraud (cheat). Counterfeiting has been a problem as long as there has been money. In ancient Rome, counterfeiting was punishable by death. Counterfeiters had their hands cut off in eleventh century England. An eighteenth century New Englander lost his ears for the crime of counterfeiting.

During the Civil War period, counterfeiting became so widespread it is estimated that by 1865 one-third of all U.S. paper money in circulation was counterfeit! The U.S. Secret Service was originally founded to combat this rash of counterfeiting. U.S. dollars were originally printed in green ink because green was a color that did not reproduce well in early photography. This prevented counterfeiting.

Photocopiers, computers, printers, and scanners have made it easier for counterfeiters to make fake bills. To make this harder, the U.S. Treasury Department has added some state-of-the-art security features. Take a look at a Series 2004 bill. The bill will say "Series 2004" just to the right of Andrew Jackson's portrait.

On the Face

1. **Portrait.** The portrait displays the most changes. It has been moved slightly off center to prevent wear. Most bills are folded in half, and the portrait on old style bills quickly became worn. The portrait has been enlarged for easy identification, and background lines

Dollars & Sense

The Problem with Counterfeiting

Counterfeiting is a problem because U.S. money is created to reflect the value of the economy. Adding bills that are not really backed by the government ends up negatively affecting our whole economy. One counterfeiter affects everyone else who is spending legal money by bringing the value of the dollar down.

are printed in fine-line patterns that are difficult to reproduce.

2. **Watermark.** A watermark—a design impressed on the paper while it is being made—is in the space to the right of the portrait. If you hold the bill up to the light, you will see the same portrait of Jackson, but without the color!

3. **Federal Reserve seal.** Rather than the seal of each of the twelve districts, one standard seal is used.

4. **Federal Reserve district letter and number.** Each of the twelve districts has its own letter and number. They are as follows: Boston, 1A; New York, 2B; Philadelphia, 3C; Cleveland, 4D; Richmond, 5E; Atlanta, 6F; Chicago, 7G; St. Louis, 8H; Minneapolis, 9I; Kansas City, 10J; Dallas, 11K; San Francisco, 12L.

5. **Serial number.** There is now an additional letter at the beginning of the number. The first letter is the series number. The second letter is the Federal Reserve district letter.

6. **Denomination.** The denomination still appears as a number in the four corners, but all the numbers are different sizes. The 20 in the left bottom corner has

MOCK UP MONEY

Fill in the missing words and notice the letters with a circle around them. When you put them in the right order you'll find out what crime has been going on since the invention of money.

In eleventh century England a person would have his _ _ ◯ _ cut off for making fake money.

A genuine portrait on a bill appears very ◯ _ _ _ ◯ and clean.

One way to tell real _ ◯ _ ◯ _ is to notice the special inks that are used.

If you get caught doing this you can go to jail for a long ◯◯ _ ◯ .

The criminals who do this need a good _ _ _ _ ◯ _ _ .

If you ever ◯ _ ◯◯ _ a three dollar bill, you know it would be one of these.

Check It Out!
You can go online to see exactly what real bills look like if you're worried you have counterfeit money.

microprinting. The microprinting must be viewed with a magnifying glass to read the print. In case you don't have a magnifying glass, it says "U.S.A. 20." The print does not photocopy clearly, so it acts as an anti-counterfeiting device. The "20" in the bottom right-hand corner is printed with a special color-shifting ink. Depending on the angle, sometimes it appears green, and sometimes it looks black. This feature is difficult to counterfeit.

7. **Microprinting**—Besides the microprinting in the numeral, microprinting is also found on the ribbon at the bottom of the portrait.

8. **Security thread**—If you hold the bill up to the light, you will see a line to the left of the Federal Reserve seal. This line is a polymer strip (thread) that has been embedded in the paper. On the thread is more microprinting that has "U.S.A. TWENTY" and a flag. The security thread appears in a different place on each denomination. When it is placed under ultraviolet light, it glows a unique color for each denomination.

9. Color shifting ink. If you look at the number 20 at the bottom right of the front of the bill, you will notice that its color changes as you move the bill.

On the Back

1. **Low-vision feature**—In the lower right hand corner, the larger "20" stands out against the light background and enables people with poorer vision to identify the denomination.

2. **Fine-line printing**—Like the background of the portrait, the background of the White House is also printed with fine lines to discourage counterfeiting.

The Treasury Department has also added some machine-readable features to the new bills to make it easier for vending machines, ATMs, and other machines to identify real bills and reject fake ones. A machine-readable feature has been added to the $20 bill so that handheld currency readers can recognize them. This makes it easier for people who are visually impaired.

Counterfeiting doesn't just happen with dollar bills. Any time someone makes a fake of something of value it is counterfeiting. Coins, checks, and credit cards are often counterfeited. Criminals also counterfeit consumer goods, such as name brand watches and purses. These are called knockoffs.

CEREAL SERIAL

Can you find the string of serial numbers hidden in this bowl of cereal?

4437294

PENNY FOR YOUR THOUGHTS

Where Do You Think Is Safe?

If you don't keep your money in a bank, where do you keep it? Why do you think that is a safe place? If we didn't have banks, where do you think people would keep their money? Why?

CHA-CHING! BANK HISTORY

Banks have been around almost as long as there has been money. Clay tablets found in Babylonia and Assyria from as long as 4,000 years ago show that people may have been loaning each other money. The Code of Hammurabi, who became king of Babylonia in 1792 B.C., included laws that have to do with banking.

When people have money, they become concerned about where to keep money. In ancient times temples were considered safe places for keeping money. Temples collected and stored large amounts of precious metals, as well as grains and other commodities. No one would dare anger the gods by trying to break into the temple treasury!

The Egyptians developed a system of banking using grains. In this system, a central grain bank in Alexandria recorded all the deposits made in Alexandria and in other state granaries. Grain owners began writing up orders so that their grain could be used to pay off debts. For example, if someone needed to pay his taxes, he wrote up an order for a certain amount of grain to be taken and given to the tax collector. Credit transfers took place in much the same way as money is transferred in banks today.

Modern Banking

Italy appears to be the birthplace of banking as we know it today. In fact, the word *bank* comes from the Italian word *banca*, which means "bench." The earliest banking transactions were done at benches or tables that were covered with green cloth. In the ninth century a bank was begun in Lombardy, a section of northern Italy. Then, in 1407, the Bank of St. George opened in Genoa, Italy. It was in business for nearly 400 years.

The Banco di Rialto, the first public bank, was started in Venice by an act of the Senate in the 1580s.

This bank acted as a depository bank. That is, customers could put money into the bank and the bank was responsible for keeping it safe. Its customers could demand the money back at any time.

The next development in banks was the exchange bank. An exchange bank worked differently from a depository bank. A customer put gold or coins into the bank, and the bank gave him a credit for it—meaning that the bank actually owed the customer money. To pay his bills, the customer could tell the bank to pay another person or business—as long as the amount of money he wanted to pay wasn't more than the amount he gave the bank. The bank kept track of how much money the customer had, and the customer could deposit money or take it out as he liked. One of the first exchange banks was the Bank of Amsterdam in the Netherlands, which opened in 1609. Finally, banks started issuing banknotes, the bills you carry in your wallet today.

Today there are many banks and banking services available.

WORDS to KNOW

UNDERWRITE: To underwrite is to take on financial responsibility for all or part of a business. It got its name because bankers at the insurance firm Lloyd's of London used to fill out a form with the borrower's information and level of risk and then write their names underneath.

- Savings and loan, commercial, and full-service banks offer a range of services including savings, checking, loans, safe deposit boxes, and investing.
- Credit unions are formed by groups of people (members) who have something in common—for example, people who work together in a large company may have a credit union. The credit union operates like a bank, but it is able to offer lower rates to its members.
- Investment banks underwrite businesses by purchasing stocks and bonds.

Today, banking is a multibillion dollar industry and is one of the most important parts of our economy. Almost all grown-ups today are paid with checks, not coins or dollar bills. A check is basically a written permission slip that says you can withdraw money from a bank—but you have to have a bank to be able to cash a check.

INTERESTED IN INTEREST?

Interest is the money a bank pays you for using your money! Sounds kind of crazy doesn't it? Someone will pay you to put money in a savings account? No way! The bank is in business to make money, so how does it make money if it is paying you more money than you put in? Simple. The bank gets to use your money for other things and it pays you for the right to do this. Banks make money through other services, one of which is lending money.

A bank lends money to an individual or a business that qualifies for a loan. That is, the bank checks to make sure the borrower can pay the money back! The bank does not just hand over the money to the borrower, either. A contract must be signed. Part of the contract covers interest. Interest is the money a borrower pays to the bank for the use of the bank's money.

The bank takes your money, pays you to be able to use it, and turns around and hands it to people who want loans. These people then pay the bank a higher amount than the bank pays you for your money. The bank uses the money it gets from loan interest and fees to cover its expenses, such as building maintenance, workers' salaries, advertising, and so on. The bank's owner hopes that enough is left over to make a profit!

CASH IT IN: CHECKING ACCOUNTS

Most kids do not get checking accounts until they get a job or go off to college. When the time comes to open

Do You Have Change for a Cow?

It is believed the first banks didn't have any money in them, or at least not money we recognize. This is because some banks existed before currency like paper and coins were invented. They would have used things that were valuable to the people at the time. Imagine bringing a goat to the bank to make a deposit!

This farmer has made a few transactions. Can you figure out what the final total is left in her account?

Multiply 7 pigs x 2 = _____

Subtract 3 cows = _____

Add 6 geese = _____

Subract 7 pigs = _____

Add 6 sheep = _____

First Account

For her birthday Sally's mother let her open her first bank account. She was very excited and started filling out the application form. Everything was going fine until she came to the space marked "name of your former bank." After a moment's thought she wrote down "Piggy."

Practice Banking

Open your own bank. Tell your mom that if she puts a dollar in your bank, you will pay her one cent per day. Then tell your dad that if he wants to borrow a dollar from your bank you will charge him five cents a day. You give your dad the money your mom put in. Your dad pays you five cents a day, but you only pay your mom one cent a day. You earn four cents per day by being the bank!

that first account, you want to be prepared for everything that is involved—finding the right account, understanding how to fill out a check, and so on.

You've probably seen checks before when your parents have written them, or maybe your grandma gave you one for your last birthday. A check acts as a substitute for cash. It means that in your grandma's bank account there is an amount of money equal to or greater than the amount she wrote on the check. The check allows the money from your grandma's bank to be transferred to you, the payee.

Checking accounts are demand deposit accounts. That is, you as the account owner can demand your money in the form of a check by transferring the funds or by making a withdrawal. When it comes time to open your first checking account, you will find there is more than one type of account to pick from.

The first kind is the personal checking account. These accounts do not pay interest on the money you keep in the bank, and you are usually charged a fee for the bank to process your checks.

A second type of checking account does pay interest. In most cases you will have to maintain a minimum balance. The bank specifies an amount of money—it could be $500 or more—that must remain in the account at all times. If you write a check that lowers your balance below the minimum, then you will not receive interest, and you will have to pay a monthly service charge.

Checks

Let's examine the front of a check.

1. **Name and address.** This information identifies the owner of the account, the drawer. The amount on the check is withdrawn from the account on the authority of the drawer.
2. **Check number.** This is located on the top right of the check. It is the number of the check as it appears

in the drawer's checkbook. Each check has a different check number. This number may also appear in magnetic ink at the bottom.

3. **Date.** You write the date the check was written.

4. **Check routing symbol.** Only banks that belong to the Federal Reserve's check clearing system will have one of these district numbers. It appears as a fraction—for example, 5-555/5550. The zero at the end means the check will be processed as soon as it gets to a Federal Reserve bank. If the last digit is a number 1 through 9, it takes a few days longer.

5. **Pay to the order of.** This is where you put the name of the person or business that is to receive the check. The person is the payee. When you fill out this section, it is best to print. Cursive tends to be harder to read. It is also recommended that you spell out the name completely to make it harder to change.

6. **Amount of the check.** This is written as a number in the box next to the line for the payee's name. For example, if you wanted to pay someone eighty-five dollars and seven cents, you would write it $85.07.

7. **Amount of the check.** On the line under the payee's name, the amount is written out in words for the dollar amount and a fraction for the cents. You would write "Eighty-five and 07/100." Fill up the whole line so that the amount can't be altered, or draw a line through any remaining space. If the numerical and written amounts are different, the bank goes by amount you wrote on this line.

8. **Name of the bank.** This is your bank, where you put the money that this check is being written against.

9. **Memo.** This space can be used to remind you what

Dollars & Sense

Bouncy Bouncy

If you write a check for more than you have in your account, the bank rejects the check and it "bounces." The bank won't pay the money, and it will also charge you a fee. Once you have a bank account, it is important to always be clear on how much money you have in it!

you wrote the check for—for example, "birthday gift."

10. **Signature.** The name should be the same as the signature on the card you signed when you opened your account. It must be written in ink so that it can't be altered.

11. **Magnetic ink character recognition.** The numbers and symbols along the bottom of the check are printed with special magnetic ink so that they can be read by machines that sort and process the checks.

12. **Routing transit number.** This is similar to the hyphenated number at the top of the check and identifies the bank for electronic transactions.

13. **Checking account number.** This identifies the account that the money will be taken (drawn) from.

14. **Check number.** This is the same as the number on the top of the check.

15. **Encoded amount.** The first bank that handles the check (either cashes it or credits it to an account) prints the amount in magnetic ink.

Checks are used because it is much easier to carry a check around than to carry large amounts of cash. Checks are also convenient because you can easily send money through the mail.

Check Out How Checks Move

How do checks work? Let's say your mom's birthday is coming up. Your dad sees an interesting book in a Bart's Better Books catalog that he knows your mom will like. He fills out the order form. He must include payment, but it is unsafe (and illegal!) to send cash through the mail, so he writes a check. He sends the $25 check to Bart's Better Books. Bart believes that your dad sent the check in "good faith." That is, your dad has enough money in his account to cover the amount of the check.

The **EVERYTHING KIDS'** Money Book

Bart deposits the check in his business bank account and sends your dad the book.

If your dad and Bart both have accounts with the same bank, it's pretty easy to transfer the money after writing a check. This kind of check is called an on-us check because all the processing is done by "us"—that is, the bank. About one-third of all checks are on-us. The remaining two-thirds of checks are called transit checks because they move between banks. Transit checks have a more complicated process. Checks may be sent to the Federal Reserve System check collection network or to a local clearinghouse (place where checks are processed).

Bart's Better Books brings your dad's check to Bank A to deposit. The money from the check is to be taken out of your dad's bank account in Bank Z. Bart's account is credited with the amount of your dad's check (+ $25). Your dad's check is then encoded with the amount to be drawn on your dad's bank account (– $25). The checks then go to the central processing area for Bank A where they are sorted. On that day, Bank A has received checks that have to go back to Banks B, C, D, X, Y, and Z. In the sorting process, the checks are separated into piles of checks for B, checks for C, checks for D, and so on.

A courier (messenger) takes the sorted checks to a central meeting place, perhaps the local clearinghouse, where couriers from many banks exchange checks. The courier from Bank A gives checks to the couriers from B, C, D, X, Y, and Z, and receives Bank A checks from each of them in exchange.

When your dad's check reaches Bank Z, the amount of his check is deducted from his account. When the next statement is mailed to him, he will receive the canceled check. Some banks now do this electronically. Instead of getting the actual check back, your dad can go online to see scanned copies of all of the checks he has written.

Sign Away

A person who receives a check and wishes to cash it or deposit it in their account must first endorse it. To endorse is to sign your name on the back of the check. By signing it, you are letting the bank know that you are the person in the "pay to the order of" line on the check. Checks can be endorsed in several ways:

1. **Blank endorsement.** A simple signature.
2. **Restrictive endorsement.** The endorser places a restriction on the transfer of money. In this case, the endorser wants the money to go into an account, rather than receive cash. You might write "For Deposit Only" under your signature, along with an account number.
3. **Special endorsement.** The endorser is giving another person the right to receive the money. Why would you do this? Say you owe $10 to your friend, John Smith. The family you mow lawns for pays you with a check for $10. Rather than cash the check, you can simply endorse it "pay to the order of John Smith."

The endorsement is important because it proves you received the check and that you are the person the check was written out to.

SUPER SAVINGS ACCOUNTS

You may already have a savings account. There are two types of simple savings accounts. One is known as a passbook account. When you sign up for this kind of account, you get a little book, a passbook, that you bring to the bank with you. Your transactions—what you put in and take out—and the interest your money earns are recorded in it. The second type is a statement account. Your transactions and interest appear on a printed record, a statement, which is mailed to you each month or quarter (every three months).

Other Savings Plans

Some other savings plans you should be aware of are money market accounts, individual retirement accounts (known as IRAs), trust accounts, and certificates of deposit. Money market accounts pay a higher rate of interest and allow you to write a limited number of checks each month, but they require you to keep a certain amount of money in the account at all times.

An IRA helps you prepare for the future. Perhaps it's a little early to begin preparing for your retirement, but it's not too early for your mom and dad! In fact, your mom and dad can even open an IRA for you. The interest earned in an IRA is not taxed by the government until after you retire. This is good because then your taxes should be lower than when you were still working.

Trust accounts are sometimes set up by parents for their children. The parents plan for the worst, their deaths. If they die before their children are old enough to take care of their own finances, then arrangements have already been made for the bank to manage the minor's (someone under legal age) money.

CDs

Certificates of deposit are also known as CDs. They are not disks that play music! A CD is a piece of paper, a certificate that is a bank's promise to repay the holder. CDs pay a higher interest rate than a regular savings account. These are some rules that the holder must follow in order to get the interest:

1. A specified amount, such as $1,000, must be deposited.
2. The money must not be taken out for a fixed amount of time—for example, six months, eighteen months, or three years. The longer the fixed amount of time, usually the better interest it pays.
3. If the money is removed before the time is up, then the holder forfeits (gives up) some of the interest! This is called a penalty.

Dollars & Sense

Savings Accounts Are Smart

If you put some of your money in a savings account, not only will you earn interest and actually increase how much you have, but you may end up spending less. If your money is in the bank, it's a lot harder to get to it than if it's just in your piggy bank. You may think twice about how badly you really want that new toy.

Fun Fact

Banks Everywhere

At the end of 2005, the United States had 7,540 banks with 75,000 branches! All the banks in the world put together were worth $60.5 trillion in 2005. That's a lot of dough!

$

INITIALLY YOURS

There are all kinds of acronyms in use today, such as ATM and TTYL. This junior bank teller has made up his own. Can you match the initials with the correct phrase?

Savings Account Withdrawal and Deposit

Saturday or Weekends Only

Interest-Free Deposit Account

Inside for Daily Account Information

Long-Term Loan

Legal Trade Union

SAWD

IFDAI

LTL

IFDA

SOWO

LTU

NSF
NSF is a real banking acronym. Can you tell what it means?

The EVERYTHING KIDS' Money Book

The bank pays more interest on a CD than a savings account because it knows it will have your money to use for a set period of time. With a savings account there is no guarantee that you won't close the account and take out all the money tomorrow!

A BANK ACCOUNT FOR YOU

Most kids don't get checking accounts until they are older, but that doesn't mean you shouldn't have a bank account. If you don't have a savings account, perhaps you should think about getting one. Why?

- A savings account pays interest on your money. Your money grows! Mold is the only thing your money will grow if you keep it under the mattress!
- Your money is safe. Can you guarantee that no one will ever get into the money you have stashed in a piggy bank? You might ask, "What about bank robbers?" Banks have insurance to cover bank robberies. "What if the bank fails and goes out of business?" If your account is kept in a Federal Deposit Insurance Corporation (FDIC) bank, it is insured up to $100,000. The FDIC is run by the U.S. government and guarantees that you will not lose your savings. The important thing is to make sure that the bank that you use is a member of the FDIC. FDIC banks usually have "Member-FDIC" notices posted where they can be easily seen. If you want to find out more, go to the "Learning Bank" at *www.fdic.gov/about/learn/learning/index.html*.
- You will develop a saving habit. Did you know that the United States is one of the worst countries in the world when it comes to saving money? In 2006 Americans saved at the rate of negative one percent. This means that as a country, Americans did not save at all. In fact, they borrowed more money than they saved!

Bank accounts can be fun! Go to the bank with a parent to open an account and they may give you a free gift, like a flashlight or a pen with the name of the bank on it. You can check your statements every month and see how quickly your money is growing!

You're never too young to open a savings account. Some parents open one for their babies as soon as they are born!

ATMs Are Everywhere

An Automated Teller Machine is usually referred to as an ATM. When you were younger you probably thought they were magic money machines. Your mom or dad put in a little plastic card, punched in some numbers, and out popped the cash!

They're a bit more complex than that! The ATM is connected to the bank's central processor (computer) by telephone lines. When a person puts her card in the machine, it reads the magnetic strip on the back and makes sure that the information relates to the bank. If it is a valid card, the person is asked to put in her "Personal Identification Number," known as a PIN. Your PIN is a secret number that only you know. This lets the machine know that the person at the machine is the owner of the account being accessed.

ATMs can do different banking functions. They can show the balance (the amount remaining in the account), make a deposit, or withdraw money. Some machines are even equipped with U.S. postage stamps—people can do their banking and buy stamps without using cash!

When a person withdraws money at an ATM, the machine checks to see that there is enough in the account. ATMs have a daily withdrawal limit, and some also deduct a fee for using the ATM. All transactions are recorded on a receipt that comes out of the machine when the transaction is finished. A bank may join a network that enables its customers to use ATMs at locations far from the home bank.

The **EVERYTHING KIDS** **Money Book**

CHARGE IT!

A charge card is different from a credit card. The charge card should be paid off every month. With a credit card you pay over a longer period of time, but you pay interest on the amount you owe, and that can add up! Make sure you read the fine print if you ever get one. There are six words hidden here. Can you spot them? The trick is knowing where to start.

I	R	P	L	A	O	O	B	O
N	E	E	T	N	A	N	O	W
T	S	N	Y	K	N	E	R	E
E	T	A	B	L	M	Y	R	D

COMPUTER CASH: ONLINE BANKING

Adults don't have to go to a bank or ATM to do a lot of their banking; a computer can help. People can move money between accounts and even pay bills online by logging onto their bank's website and telling it what they want to do. This is called electronic funds transfer, or EFT. There is a nationwide communications/computer network where a large number of banks and businesses transfer money between accounts.

For example, an employee is paid weekly by check. The check must be brought to the bank to be deposited. Between the time the employee receives the check and takes it to the bank, the check could be lost or stolen. With EFT, the employee is able to have the amount of the paycheck credited to his checking or savings account immediately. This is referred to as direct deposit. The amount credited is available right away so

that the employee can write checks or withdraw money. The employee gives the employer written permission to do this. Rather than having to write out a check and have it signed each week, the employer simply arranges to have the money transferred from the business account to the employee's account. Both employer and employee benefit.

Bank customers can also go to their bank's website and access their bank records. They can see what checks they wrote and what deposits they made. On this site, people can tell the bank's computer to pay a company electronically. If a person gets a bill from the electric company, he can go to his bank's website and have the bank send the payment to the electric company's bank electronically. He doesn't have to write a check and he knows the payment was made right away.

PLASTIC

You've probably heard credit cards referred to as "plastic." The reason for this is obvious—they are made of plastic! Ask your parents how many credit or debit cards they have. You might be surprised at how many they have in their wallets!

How Credit Works

Before we talk about plastic credit cards, let's talk about credit itself. Credit is an arrangement between the seller and the buyer. The seller agrees to trust the buyer to purchase something, leave with it, and pay for it later. The seller is rewarded for her trust by prompt payment, or, if payment is not on time, the seller charges an additional amount called interest.

Imagine that you want to buy your friend's bag of

marbles. You didn't bring any money with you when you went to her house, so you tell her you will pay her for it on Tuesday when you see her again. She gives you the marbles and you take them home, then you pay her the next time you see her. She has just given you credit. Now, if you forget to pay her back when you see her, she may not be happy and if you want to buy her bouncy ball next, she might decide you are not a good credit risk and refuse to let you take it without paying.

There are different kinds of credit arrangements. One is the installment plan method of buying. Say your parents want to buy an expensive item such as a new dishwasher. The store allows them to make a down payment; that is, they pay a certain percentage of the total price when they make the purchase. Then, over a period of months or years, your parents pay off the rest of the purchase cost, plus interest. If they fail to make the payments, the seller gets to take the item back (repossess it) and sell it to someone else.

Credit Cards

Charge accounts are credit issued by individual stores or chains. These accounts come with credit cards that are only good at that particular store or one of its branches. Major credit cards (MasterCard, Visa, Discover, and American Express are the most popular) allow adults to buy goods and services at any business that accepts that particular credit card. Some parents get an extra credit card from their account that they allow their teenagers to use.

Credit and credit cards are not given to everyone. Businesses carefully screen out people who are a credit risk. How do they do this? They have a person fill out forms listing their assets, employer, yearly income, credit information (such as other credit cards owned), loans, and so on.

Adults who use credit cards must be careful with them. They should not share their account number with anyone and always check their bills carefully to be sure they charged everything that is listed.

WORDS to KNOW

ASSET: An asset is anything you own that can be converted into cash to cover your debt.

Dollars & Sense

Credit Problems

If you've ever seen your parent use a credit card, you know how easy it is to swipe and go. Lots of people spend too much with their credit cards because they forget they need to have actual money to pay the credit card bill when it comes. Credit cards can make buying things easier, but never forget that they have to be paid off!

PENNY FOR YOUR THOUGHTS

Are Gift Cards Great?

Do you enjoy getting gift cards? Some people like them because you don't have to worry about whether something fits or if the person likes it—they can go to the store and pick out their own gift. Is it exciting to open a present with a gift card in it, or would you rather open a present that is something you can use right away?

Debit Cards

Some ATM cards may also be used as debit cards. Adults can use a debit card instead of cash at stores and gas stations. When the adult swipes the card in the card reader and puts in the PIN, their checking account is immediately adjusted to reflect the amount of the debit. In other words, the money is removed from the bank account.

Some schools use debit cards in the cafeteria. Your parents put a certain amount of money into your account. You are given a debit card to take to lunch. Each time you buy lunch, a drink, or a snack, the cost of the food is deducted from the debit account. When it is empty, your parents have to add more money to the account. It can be a lot easier than making sure you have lunch money every day, but if you lose the debit card, you lose all the money on it!

Gift Cards

You've probably received a gift card as a present from someone. A gift card looks like a credit card, but it can only be used at one store. The person who gave you the gift paid the store a certain amount of money (like $20 or $50). This money was credited to the gift card. When you go into the store and use the card, the price of the things you buy are deducted from the account. When you use it, it's all gone.

You might have returned something to a store and gotten a plastic card with a store credit on it. The price of the thing you returned is credited to the account for the card. You use it just like a gift card. If you lose a gift card or store credit, you lose all the money on that card.

HOW GROWN-UPS EARN MONEY

One or both of your parents probably heads out to work every day. Adults need to earn money to pay for their home, car, clothes, food, and everything they buy. The average adult in the United States works 39.5 hours every week at a job. Almost all adults who want jobs are able to find them. About 4.7% of adults (almost five out of every 100) are unemployed. The average U.S. adult earns about $26,000 a year. That might sound like a lot of money, but once you understand how much stuff costs (see Chapter 7 for more information), you'll see that it isn't all that much.

Most adults have jobs to earn their money, but there are other ways people get money.

- **Interest.** Chapter 4 talks about how money you put in the bank earns interest. Many adults earn some interest on their money.
- **Benefits.** Many adults get benefits with their jobs, things such as paid health insurance, cars to use for business, membership in clubs, and so on. These things are not money paid directly to employees, but they are things employees do not have to buy for themselves, which means they can keep more of the money they earn.
- **Owning a Business.** A person who owns a business usually runs the business as her job. A business can be a huge corporation, or it can be a small company run out of a home.
- **Investments.** People can buy shares of companies they think will make money and share part of the profit. Chapter 6 talks about this.
- **Luck.** Some people win money by playing the lottery.
- **Gifts.** Gifts of money are another way adults can get money.
- **Inheritance.** An inheritance is when a relative or friend dies and leaves money to his loved ones after his death. Some of the wealthiest people are rich because their families are.

- **Extra Income.** Adults can also earn money by selling things they own, working extra jobs, or making and selling things.

Making money is something that adults spend a lot of their time doing.

A+ ALLOWANCE

Many kids receive an allowance from their parents. An allowance is, quite simply, an amount of money given on a regular basis—in most cases, weekly. If you do not get an allowance, you might be able to convince your parents to give you one. Your parents believe in education, right? Well, working with an allowance teaches kids responsibility and the value of money.

Many parents are afraid that kids will not spend their allowance wisely. You may make some foolish spending choices, but if you do, the decision to do so is your own and hopefully you will learn from your mistakes. Much of learning occurs through trial and error—ask any scientist! Explain to your parents that money is something you will have to deal with for the rest of your life. It is better that you make your mistakes early on rather than later when the stakes may be higher! Explain that you will have a family someday and you need to know how to manage your money. Not everything is taught at school!

Allowance Amount

How much should you get? That all depends on your family circumstances, but perhaps a good negotiating point would be to suggest $1 for every year of age. For example, if you are eight years old, you would get $8 a week. If you are 14, you would get $14.

Fun Facts

Money for Parents
If your mom or dad is one of the 5.5 million parents who stay home with their kids, you might think he or she doesn't work. Wrong! It would take $138,000 a year to pay someone to do all the things a stay at home parent does!

Who Gets an Allowance?
A survey by the site *www.kidsmoney.org* found that 74 percent of kids get allowances. Of those who get allowances, 66 percent have to do chores to be paid and 54 percent of kids who get allowances have to save part of it.

$

Earning Power

Doctors, dentists, heads of companies, and airline pilots are the jobs that pay the most in the United States. Why do you think people in these jobs are paid so much? Are there other jobs you think should be in this group? Why?

TRY THIS

Yesterday's Allowance

Ask your parents what they got for an allowance when they were your age. It probably doesn't sound like a lot, but remember that the value of money changes over time. Go to *www.bls.gov/cpi* and click on "Inflation Calculator." You can put in the amount your mom or dad got at your age and find out how much that would be worth today.

If you'd like something more scientific, why not do a study? Write down everything you buy for yourself and everything that is bought for you by your parents in a one- or two-week period. Don't leave anything off your list—write down the twenty-five cents you put in the gum machine at the grocery store, the money you spend for lunch at school, the $15 your parents spend for your karate lessons, and the cost of a new pen and some notebook paper. Don't forget to include the money you put into the church collection basket or the money you used to buy your friend a birthday present. At the end of the week, add up the costs. Has it been a typical week? Will your expenses be roughly the same from week to week?

Go over the list with your parents. Decide what expenses are your parents' responsibility and what are yours. Perhaps they can pay for your school lunches, but you should pay for the popsicle you get on the way home from school. Once you've figured out how much money you need to pay for things every week, consider building in an additional amount for savings.

Is the amount you need met by the dollar-for-each-year-of-age formula suggested earlier? If not, what would be a good figure? Discuss it with your parents.

Sweat for Cents

Another way to negotiate an allowance is to discuss chores. Here again it helps to make up a chart of a week's worth of chores. A simple chart would have the days of the week across the top. Under each day, list the chores you have done. Do you put out the trash three times a week? If so, under Monday, Wednesday, and Friday, write in "put out trash." If you set the table for dinner every day, write it in every day. Do you mow the lawn or shovel the driveway? List these things as seasonal tasks at the bottom of the page so that you and your parents can use them to get a total picture of what you do. After the week is up, look at the list with your

PAYBACK TIME

All the kids at the bottom of the page have borrowed some money, but now it's time to pay it back. First they have to find the right person to pay it to. Can you connect the borrower with the right lender?

Wise Words
"If you would be wealthy, think of saving
as well as getting."

—Benjamin Franklin

parents. They may be surprised to see how much you really do around the house, or you may be embarrassed at how little you do!

In any case, you and your parents need to decide which of those things are just "good family member" chores and which are a little extra and deserve an allowance. It could be doing the dishes every day and feeding the cats, even if you hate the cats! Or, your parents may decide just to give you the money! You could also volunteer to do more around the house if they will pay you for it.

Strings Attached

Are there any other rules attached to your allowance? Probably. Once you start on an allowance you may have to pay for all your expenses—that is, you don't get extra money to go to a movie or a concert. If you can't pay for it out of your allowance or your savings, you don't go. So if your friends have big plans to attend the opening of a new movie three weeks from now, start saving part or all of your allowance for your ticket (and some popcorn, of course)!

Some parents feel that putting part of the allowance money into savings or investments will encourage setting long-term goals. It won't be long before you're looking at colleges! You may be required to put "untouchable" money in the bank every week.

Will you receive cash or a check that will require you to go to the bank each week? Will your parents hold onto your allowance money for you? If so, how will you get it if you need it?

TWINS OR NOT

These twins are getting their allowance. But maybe they're not really twins. Can you find the eight differences between them?

Talk it over. If you and your parents want to be satisfied with your plan, then it is important that you all come to an agreement beforehand about what is expected. Put in writing what you will receive each week, on what day you will receive it, and what you are responsible for doing. You may even wish to put in a paragraph stating that the agreement is subject to renegotiation in six months or a year. If both you and your parents sign the agreement, you have made a contract—just like in the real world of business!

Although we've been talking about weekly allowances, you can make other arrangements. If your mom or dad gets paid once every two weeks, then it might make sense for you to be paid on the same basis. Some kids are paid monthly to give them practice in setting up and living within a budget.

WORK FOR IT!

Getting an allowance is great, but sometimes an allowance isn't enough money to let you buy all the things you want. If you need more money, you could earn it. Look at the chores you do. Is there something that needs to be done around the house or yard that doesn't fall into the category of required chores? Maybe your parents want to paint the hallway. You could do the job of removing the wallpaper, washing the walls, taping off the trim, and so on. Discuss with your parents what would be a fair wage for the job, then offer to do it. If they agree, decide on a time for you to do the work. If your dad plans on painting on Sunday, promise to do the prep work Saturday afternoon, even if it means giving up a trip to the mall with your friends.

Are you at least fourteen years old? If not, then getting a "regular" job may not be possible. Many states require that you be fourteen to work unless you work on

The EVERYTHING KIDS Money Book

the family farm. In most states you can deliver newspapers when you are twelve. How can you find out about the rules in your state? A school guidance counselor will be able to help you. She can tell you about working papers, the number of hours you are allowed to work per week during the school year, and so on. Child labor laws regulate the work young people can do to ensure they stay healthy and get a good education.

What are some jobs you can get without having working papers? Babysitting, house cleaning, and yard work are all popular with kids. Others include washing cars (great for groups that need to make money!), dog walking, or pet sitting.

Look into babysitting courses offered by the local American Red Cross chapter, the YMCA, your county extension, or the local recreation department. Parents will appreciate the fact that you have been trained, and you will be better prepared for emergencies. Kids who

WORK AND PLAY

Julio has a summer job so he can buy something he really wants, but he has to work hard for it. Can you figure out what Julio wants by filling in the missing letters?

R		T	A	S		W	F	R				
A	T	I	D	T	G	H	O	A	P	B	L	B
B	R	S	D	A	R	A	L	N	I	R	O	R
I	D	U	D	L	D	E	O	E	L	K	E	A
T	E	E		E	E		W	R	O	E	L	T
					S				W	N	Y	H

are not old enough to babysit can become helpers. A helper entertains the children so that the parents can get some work or housework done! Babysitting is not just for girls! Parents love to hire older boys to babysit.

Yard work or cleaning out garages and attics are great jobs if you like physical activity. For jobs like these you may have to invest in some equipment such as rakes, shovels, and work gloves. Often, though, the person hiring you will have the equipment for the job. A word of warning—never accept a job that would put you in danger, such as trimming branches near electrical lines.

Here are a few more jobs you may not have thought of:

- **Computer installation and instruction.** You could set up computers and printers for adults you know who've bought new computers but don't know the first thing about using them!
- **Web-page design.** Kids who know HTML (hypertext mark-up language) can help small businesses or organizations set up their websites.
- **Word processing.** If you've grown up with a computer, you've probably got the keyboarding down pat!
- **Housesitting.** A neighbor could hire you to water his plants and bring in his newspaper and mail while he is away.
- **Volunteer positions.** Nonpaying jobs, such as volunteering at the animal shelter, are valuable for the experience you get. You learn to follow instructions, work according to a schedule, and interact with the public. These are all skills that you can apply to a paying job later. And don't overlook the fact that if you prove yourself to be a good worker in a volunteer position, you may get first notice when a paying position opens up!

A DOLLAR AND A DREAM

An entrepreneur is a person who sets up a business. Have you considered starting up a business? Selling lemonade from the end of your driveway is a good start, but committing to a long-term plan and working hard to meet your goals is how you start a successful business.

First you start with an idea or an interest. Do you enjoy helping your dad plan for family barbecues? Shopping for matching paper plates and cups? Making up a menu of special treats? You might want to think about a party business and offer your service to other parents. Expanding on the party idea, you could think about entertaining little kids at birthday parties. Would you like to clown around and get dressed up in costumes? Taking the idea one step further, how about making twisted balloon sculptures? Could you learn to make balloon animals and silly hats? Little kids love to watch balloon animals being made. And they love it even more if they get to take a balloon home!

Business Plan Basics

So now you've got an idea. You can set up a business entertaining little kids at parties by making balloon animals. Next you need a plan—a business plan. Consider your situation. Do you have the time to do everything that is involved? Will it interfere with your schoolwork? Will your parents approve? Think about the balloon animal business. You'll need to learn special skills and practice your act. Should you make or buy a costume, or will a silly bow tie and a simple balloon hat be enough? How about a catchy name for your business? Where will you advertise your services? What will you charge your customers?

Before you start on any of these, you want to do a market survey. What's a market survey? It's a study that will tell you if there is a need for your business in the area you live. Wouldn't it be horrible if you spent time and money setting up your business and then found out that there are twenty other businesses in your town that do the exact same thing?

Rule of Thirds
If you don't have a plan in your family for how you must spend your allowance, you could follow the rule of thirds—spend a third, save a third, and give a third away. Some kids follow the rule of fourths—spend a fourth, save a fourth, give a fourth away, and invest the last fourth.

Start in your own neighborhood. Are there many kids ages eight and under? Ask the parents of these children if they ever hire entertainment for their kids' parties. Who have they hired? Were they happy with what they got? Would they be interested in balloon entertainment? What would they be willing to pay for someone to keep the kids amused for about forty-five minutes?

Get out the yellow pages. Look up *clowns* or *parties* and see if there are any listings for *children's entertainment*. Go to the public library. There may be a children's services directory that lists entertainment services in your area. (If there is a directory, make a note of the publisher. If your business is a success you could advertise in the directory!) Do an Internet search for party entertainment in your area.

Okay, your market survey has left you feeling that there's definitely a need in your town for your service. What's next? Training. Having seen a balloon twister at work and thinking, "It looks easy enough," doesn't mean balloon twisting is easy! Again, go to the public library and look for books on balloons and/or clowning or visit some websites about it. Remember how the people you've seen making balloon animals always kept up a steady stream of talk? Take out a few books on jokes or bookmark some websites.

Start-Up Cash

You'll need start-up money to get your business going. You may have to buy a balloon twisting book to bring with you to parties. Also necessary are a supply of balloons and perhaps a small pump if your lung power isn't great! You might need to buy some clothes to create your entertainer outfit. Look at your own savings to see if you have enough. If not, discuss with your parents if they will loan you the money until your first paying gig. To add a professional touch to your arrangement, put the promise of repayment in writing. Your parents will realize that you are serious and may be more willing to help you.

Getting Ready

While you're busy practicing, you can also be thinking about a name for your business. How does "Balloon Buddy" sound? Maybe you're a "Balloon Artist"! Ask your parents and friends what they think of your name choice.

After much practice, you will be able to tell if this business idea will really work. If you feel confident enough to perform in front of an audience, try out your act on your relatives and friends first. Then you could volunteer at your local library or at a day-care center. If you do well, the parents of kids at the library will want to hire you for their kids' upcoming birthday parties. You could also offer to do a party for free to get some experience.

Next, think about other ways you will get the word out about your business. You could create a website and send e-mails to people you know to tell them about your business. You could print out fliers and hand them out to parents at the town T-ball game. You can easily design a flier on a computer if you're not artistically inclined. Make copies on colored paper—brightly colored fliers attract attention on bulletin boards. Ask to post your fliers on bulletin boards at the public library, your school, your church, the grocery store, and the town recreation department. Make sure you put in your telephone number so that a customer can get in touch with you! Don't put your rate on the flier. This allows you room to negotiate. You may be willing to charge the Daisy Girl Scouts less, or nothing at all, if it means more people (potential customers) will see you perform. You'll also feel good about doing a charitable deed.

The library or community center might let you hang up a sign. The most important thing you can do is talk about your business with people that you meet.

Fun Fact

Doggie Banks?

We have piggy banks, but not doggie banks or ostrich banks. Why? The term *piggy bank* comes from a reddish clay used for making pottery in the Middle Ages, called pygg. Money was often kept in jars or pots made of pygg. This type of pottery was called piggery, which also means a place where pigs are kept. The words got mixed up, and by the eighteenth century people were making pig-shaped banks!

Price Point

At this point you will need to be ready to tell a potential customer your price. You got some ideas of what the market will bear—that is, what people are willing to pay—from your market survey. A parent may help by telephoning a professional entertainer and asking for her rates. Since you are new at the business, you should be willing to be paid a whole lot less! Professional rates are something for you to shoot for—a business goal.

Where Is Your Business Going?

This might be a good time to talk about business goals. Entrepreneurs set goals for their businesses. Goals should be realistic. In the balloon twisting business it wouldn't do you any good to set a goal to earn a million dollars in your first year. A more realistic goal would be to book one party a month in your first year. This is a reachable goal.

Businesses also prepare mission statements—that is, a brief explanation of what they are trying to do. For the balloon business it could be something like, "to provide comical entertainment for children ages four to eight by making balloon animals." Try it—write a mission statement for whatever business you would consider starting up. If you cannot do it easily, then perhaps you don't really know what it is you are trying to do. You may need to rethink your business!

Contract

You're ready to go, right? Wrong! Have you thought about a contract? It's a business! You should spell out exactly what your customers will receive. A contract should include the date, start time and place, and how long the entertainment will last. Other agreed upon conditions like "each child in attendance will receive two animals" should be included. The price you are charging and how you expect payment—for example, "$25 cash or check on the day of performance"—should be a part of your contract. You will also need to have a place where both you and the customer can sign and add the date.

Business Sense

The best form of advertising is free—word of mouth. If you do a good job and someone recommends you to another person, then you've been given free promotion! If a customer tells you you've done a good job, ask him if you may use him as a reference. A reference is another person's word that you can do the job well.

Follow these rules to make sure you have satisfied customers:

- Be on time. Show up ready to work every time. Have everything you need and get right to it.
- Look good. No matter what kind of job you are doing, show up looking ready to do it. A neat appearance inspires confidence.
- Be complete. Finish your job every time. Know exactly what your customer expects and deliver it. If you don't do a complete job, you won't be hired again.
- Be polite. Say "please" and "thank you" and speak politely to everyone you are working with. Look people in the eye when you talk to them and speak loudly and clearly so people can hear you.
- Be safe. Make sure you go over safety procedures before taking any job. Know how to reach the person you are working for, where to find a phone, and make sure your parents approve of where you're going and what you're doing.

Following these tips will ensure you are hired again and again!

BOOKKEEPING: Bookkeeping is an accounting system that lets you keep track of your income and expenses.

The Bottom Line

Finally, the day arrives. You show up on time. You and the kids have a good time. You get paid your $25. Now it's time to see if you've made any money.

"But," you say, "I just made $25." Yes, you did, but did you remember to subtract your expenses? If you subtract your expenses from your income, you find that you made -$1.45 for your first gig! A negative amount is known as a loss.

Have you failed? No, of course not. You did a good job. Two mothers asked for your flier and a dad booked you on the spot! Give yourself a pat on the back!

You have to remember that some of your expenses will last through all of your jobs. The second gig is easier. You have a larger audience this time, so you have to buy more balloons, but you don't have to buy another book or a new outfit for yourself! You get paid $25. Now have you made money? This time when you subtract your expenses from your income you find that you made $14.95! A profit!

Your business has begun. Now you should update your business plan so that you can continue in business. Include advertising, continued training (you have to keep wowing your customers by twisting new animals), setting up a system of bookkeeping, paying taxes, and seeking free publicity. If you do a free show, ask the group you do it for to invite the local newspaper. You'll get your picture in the paper and will make yourself known to more potential customers. And if you get a few parties signed up in advance, you may be able to buy your balloons in a larger quantity so they'll cost you less per balloon.

After a period of about six months, sit down and evaluate your business. Is it going according to your expectations? Are you happy doing the work? Do your losses outnumber your profits? Are you keeping up with your schoolwork? Your social life? At this point you could decide to throw in the towel and quit. You've given it your best, so there is nothing to be sorry about. In the adult world, 70 to 80 percent of new businesses do not make it beyond the first year!

If you are enjoying your work, meeting new people, and making a little money, then you may decide to keep going. Good for you! Or, maybe you've been successful but you've outgrown your business idea and would like to try some other business. Either way, setting up a business has been a valuable learning experience—you learned a skill, you increased your self-confidence, and you proved to your parents that you can see a project through.

THANK YOU! GETTING GIFTS OF MONEY

As you get older, relatives might have a harder time figuring out what to get you for your birthday or for the holidays. Sometimes an aunt will get you the same thing year after year after year. Just because you liked the fake-fur bear slippers she got you when you were four, she thinks you will still like them when you are fourteen.

Kids always appreciate a gift of money, but many grown-ups don't like to give money because they're afraid it will be frittered away. Here's what you can do. Is there something that you need to save for? Spending money for two weeks at soccer camp? An MP3 player? Do some consumer homework. Figure out how much you will need. How long will you have to save? When is the camp payment due?

If you want the MP3 player, check out a consumer magazine such as *Consumer Reports* for reliability ratings, or do an Internet search. Read the Sunday ads for sale prices and check different websites. Learn how to comparison shop. Ask your friends if they are happy with

Dollars & Sense

Giving Thanks

Relatives who live far away may send you checks as birthday or holiday gifts. Take the time to write a thank-you note or e-mail to the giver. Just saying "thanks" isn't enough. You could mention what you plan to use the money for so the giver feels like he is part of your purchase.

Dollars & Sense

Don't Be Debt Dumb

It can seem really easy to borrow $20 here and $10 there from family and friends. The problem is you have to pay it back. If you keep borrowing, you will owe so much money that you will have to use all your allowance or earnings to pay it back. Instead, only borrow money when you absolutely have to and when you can comfortably work out a plan to pay it back.

the MP3 players they have. Listen when they tell you that the sound of the XYZ brand isn't good, or that you'll have to recharge the battery every ten hours with the ABC brand. Decide on the best MP3 player for you. How much will it cost? How much do you already have? How much more do you need?

Tell the gift givers about your plans. Maybe if your aunt knows what a mature shopper you are, she might want to help you out with something green for your well-thought-out purchase, rather than something fuzzy for your feet! You can also always ask relatives for gift cards.

Money gifts for college are frequently given to an older kid. Since you have several years before you're ready to attend college, you can put these gifts into a 529 plan or save them until you have enough for a certificate of deposit—see Chapter 4. Investing the "for college" gift money is another option, but with investment comes risk. See Chapter 6 for more information about investing and 529 plans.

PRETTY PLEASE? BORROWING MONEY

Another way to get money is to borrow it. Adults borrow money often. An adult can go to a bank and apply for a loan. The bank looks to see if the person has a job, pays his bills on time, and is a good credit risk. If so, the bank loans the money. The loan is usually for a specific amount of time, such as five years or thirty years. The person borrowing the money must make monthly payments to the bank. These payments are used to repay the amount of the loan and to pay the interest the bank is charging (see Chapter 4 for information about interest). Adults often borrow money to buy homes and cars. A home loan is called a mortgage.

ATTACK THE TAX

Taxes have been collected ever since Roman times. One of the most famous tax protesters was Lady Godiva, who rode through town without any clothes on. She wanted her husband to reduce the taxes he charged the peasants. These peasants look like they're going to have trouble getting back inside the castle walls. Can you help them through the maze?

Tax the Queen!

In 1992 Queen Elizabeth began to pay taxes for the first time in history in a bid to bring her closer to the people.

When an adult borrows money for a home or car, she agrees that if she doesn't pay back the loan, the bank can take the home or the car. This is called repossession. Usually a bank will sell the home or car and use the money to pay off the rest of the loan.

You've probably borrowed money from your parents or friends. If there is a big purchase you want to make, such as hockey gear or cool new shoes, you could ask a parent if you could borrow the money. When you do this, create a plan so that your parent knows you are serious about paying it back. If you want to borrow $50, you could plan to pay back $5 a week. Your loan would be paid off in 10 weeks. Most parents don't charge their kids interest, but a sibling or a friend might. Your brother might agree to lend you $20 if you pay him back $22 total. He would earn $2 in interest.

OWING UNCLE SAM

Everyone who earns money must pay a portion of it to the government as income tax. The money the government collects through taxes is used to pay for the services the government provides, such as schools, hospitals, postal service, police, military, road repairs, parks, fire department, ambulance, courts, and much more. The United States tax system is a sliding scale system. The more you earn, the more you pay.

Kids have to pay taxes too. If you have a job and earn more than $850 a year (this amount changes every year), your parents will help you file an income tax return (a document showing how much you earned and how much you owe in taxes) and pay a portion of it to the government. If you earned investment income more than $1,700, you have to file a return. If you have a job and your employer withholds (takes out) taxes from your pay, you also must file a return. Tax returns and any money that is owed have to be filed by April 15 of the next year. So if you earn enough money this year to

The EVERYTHING KIDS' Money Book

have to pay taxes, your return will be due on April 15 of next year.

Income tax is serious business. There is an entire government agency called the Internal Revenue Service (IRS) that is in charge of collecting taxes and making sure people pay the correct amount. If you owe taxes and don't pay them, you will have to pay fines. Some adults who don't pay their taxes for many years or who lie on their tax returns end up going to jail for their crimes.

Chapter 6

MONEY MAKES MONEY

THE AMAZING GROWING DOLLAR

If you wanted to start up a leaf raking business but needed money to buy tools and do some advertising, your mom might agree to invest some money in your company. She might agree to give you $50, which you would not have to repay, as long as you shared part of your profits with her. She gives you the $50 which allows you to buy good tools and do a lot of advertising. You get a lot of work and start raking in the dough. You pay her ten cents for every dollar you make. The better your business does, the more money she makes.

This is how investing works. People invest money in companies. The money allows the companies to grow. As the companies grow, they pay money to their investors.

Investing is a neat way to make money without doing any work. However, it can also be a way to lose your money quickly! If you fell out of your tree house and sprained your wrist and could not rake any more leaves, your mom wouldn't get any profit from your business. She would have made a bad investment. Investments can be good or bad, so it is important to be knowledgeable before you invest your money.

A 200-year study of the stock market showed that the average yearly return (yearly increase in value) for stocks was 9.5 percent. Some stocks earn more and some earn less, but on average this is how the stock market grows.

Are You the Investing Type?

Are you the type of kid who can be an investor? There are several things you must think about before seriously considering investing. Examine your own personality. Do you find the idea of buying stock in a new company that may (or may not) come up with the next big electronics miracle exciting? You could make some real money! But what if the company you invest in fails and you lose your money? Would you be very upset? How much money can you invest? Based on your income, allowance, gifts, babysitting earnings, and so on, if you can set aside even $100 a year, it might be worth it to you to invest this money.

What are your goals? Do you want to buy Christmas presents for your friends and family? If so, then investing is not the way to go. To see the results of your investments, you must be willing to be patient and wait. If you are planning on going to college in another eight years, then investing your $100 a year may be something for you and your parents to consider. You wouldn't be able to pay for your whole college education, but you just might be able to cover the cost of your books or set up an account for spending money while you're in college.

Many kids don't realize the amount of time and effort that goes into investing. You earn your money by taking on the job of investing, but overnight success is rare. If you're looking to get rich quick, forget it. One of the keys to investing is patience—think five years or more! Also, you must remember that by investing you are tying up your money. If you want your money where you can get at it easily, then perhaps a savings account is the best option for you.

Stock Market Secrets

A stock is a share in a business. Here are some things you should know about stocks:

- When a new company feels a need to expand, it may not have the money to do so. A decision is made to "go public." By going public, a company decides to sell shares (stock) in its business. The people in charge of the business now have to report to the shareholders, the people who bought stock, who each own a tiny part of the company.
- The initial public offering (IPO) is the first time stock is sold by that company. Investment bankers buy up the stock

WORDS to KNOW

DIVIDEND: A dividend is the money that is paid to investors as a share of earnings in a company.

and then are responsible for selling it. It is interesting that this is the only time the company makes money from selling its stock. From this point on, the buying and selling of stock is in the hands of the investment bank and brokers.

- The shares of stock are sold to investors. Investors come from all walks of life. They may also include groups other than individuals—for example, institutions or other businesses.
- Each shareholder may vote at an annual meeting to elect directors of the business.
- Each share has an equal vote, but the more shares a person owns, the greater the number of votes the person has.
- Businesses that make a profit pay dividends to their stockholders. Those companies that make high dividend payments to their stockholders every year are called income stocks. People buy income stocks so that they can depend on a steady income from their shares.
- Some companies may use profits to make improvements to the business. They may not pay dividends, or if they do, they are small. The stock for these companies is called growth stock. Growth stocks are expected to grow in value because the company has improved or expanded and can go on to make more money.
- Stocks are traded on exchanges, special places where stocks are bought and sold. The New York Stock Exchange (NYSE) and the American Stock Exchange (AMEX) are the primary exchanges in the United States. The National Association of Securities Dealers Automatic Quotation System (NASDAQ) sells stocks that are not listed with an exchange. These are called over-the-counter (OTC).
- A person who buys and sells stocks for a client is called a broker.

When people talk about the stock market, they mean the entire industry of selling and buying stocks. The stock market is deeply tied to our economy. When the economy is doing well, prices of stocks go up. The stock market can also affect the economy. If the stock market

prices fall, the economy can be negatively affected.

People make money from stocks, not just from the dividends. Some people buy stocks and wait for them to increase in value. When they do, they sell them for a profit. The key is to guess which stocks will increase in value and to sell them before their value goes down. If you want to get the money you put into your stocks back out, you must call your broker and have her sell them. You will get the price they are trading for that day, which could be higher or lower than you paid. The stock market can be a risky business.

KEEPING TRACK OF STOCKS

A good way to explore the world of the stock market is to make your first investment with imaginary money!

Give yourself $1,000 (or more; it's not real!) and think about a product you are interested in. It can be your favorite candy bar, soda, running shoes, or computer software.

Find out who makes the product. For example, let's say you just had Rice Krispies for breakfast. Look at the box to find that Kellogg Company makes the cereal. You could also choose a store or product you like, such as Dreamworks Animation or Hershey. Go to the financial section of a large newspaper to find the stock or stocks you are considering.

Now you need to learn how to read a stock listing. Each company has its own symbol. The symbol is usually an abbreviation of a company's name. If you don't know your company's symbol, you can look it up. If you open up your newspaper, you will see pages and pages of letters and numbers in very tiny print. Don't be scared away! Each stock listing is very short. Let's take a look at our three examples.

STOCK	SYM	CLOSE	NET CHG
Drmwrks Anmt A	DWA	31.08	0.35
Hershey	HSY	37.01	−0.61
Kellogg	K	51.68	−0.33

You can probably figure out what most of that means, but here's a brief explanation.

- **STOCK.** This is the name of the company. Sometimes it's shortened when the name is too long. That's what happened to Dreamworks!
- **SYM.** This is short for symbol and it refers to the company's ticker symbol. A ticker is an old-fashioned way of reporting stock transactions. Symbols and prices used to be transmitted by telegraph on long skinny pieces of paper called ticker tape. Today, this information is transmitted electronically through computers and networks.

- **CLOSE.** This was the price of the stock when the market closed the day before.
- **NET CHG.** This stands for *net change*. It is the comparison of the price at the close of the day with the price at the close of the previous day's trading. If the price went down, it is shown by a minus sign (–). If the price went up, it is shown by a plus sign (+) or by nothing at all. Any listing in bold print shows a share that has had a change of 5 percent or more. How did the stocks in our example do yesterday?

You can also find these stocks online at *www.amex.com*, *www.nasdaq.com*, any major newspaper site, and even sites like Yahoo! Finance (*finance.yahoo.com*). All of these sites have different ways of reporting the stock prices, but here is an example of what you might see.

The online listings can be a little bit tricky to read since there's so much information! But once you know what everything means, it's very easy.

	DWA	HSY	K
Last Sale	$29.84	$37.15	$51.75
Change	1.25 ▼ 4.02%	0.14 ▲ 0.38%	0.07 ▲ 0.14%
Previous Close	$31.09	$37.01	$51.68
Open	$29.32	$37.36	$52.00
1y Target Est.	$32.50	$33.00	$58.50
Today's High/Low	$30.29/$28.84	$37.66/$36.96	$52.00/$51.53
52 Wk High/Low	$34.99/$21.25	$51.78/$33.54	$56.89/$46.25
P/E Ratio	12.92	19.15	18.48
Share Volume	1,355,254	944,940	2,055,405
Avg Vol.	938,725	1,728,710	2,085,010
Div & Yield	N/A (N/A)	1.19 (3.20%)	1.24 (2.40z%)

- **Last sale.** This is the price for the most recent sale. One of the great things about the Internet is that it can let you know about things almost as soon as they happen. You can check for updates on how your stock is doing throughout the day. If you only got the newspaper, you'd only be able to see the price at the end of the day.

- **Change.** This shows both the amount and the percent of change since the last day's close.
- **Previous close.** This shows the price for this stock the last time the market closed.
- **Open.** This is how much the stock sold for when the market first opened today.
- **1 year target estimate.** Just as meteorologists forecast the weather, stock experts (who like to be called analysts) use complicated mathematical formulas to help them guess how much the value of a stock will change in the next year.
- **Today's high/low.** This shows the highest and lowest amounts that buyers paid for this stock today.
- **52 week high/low.** There are 52 weeks in a year. The high and low are the highest and lowest prices the stocks have been traded for in the past year.
- **P/E ratio.** *P/E* stands for "price to earnings." The previous closing stock price is divided by the earnings per share. The higher the number, the better the stock is doing— usually. To really tell how your stock is doing, compare its P/E ratio with those of other companies that do similar work. For example, you'll want to compare Kellogg's P/E ratio with General Mills'.
- **Share volume.** This shows the number of shares that have been traded today.
- **Average volume.** This is the average number of shares that are traded.
- **Dividend and yield.** The first number is the estimated dividend to be paid per share. The percentage is the yield. It is the dividend divided by the price per share, and it shows what percentage of your investment you will receive in dividends. Not all companies pay dividends. That's why this category says "N/A" for Dreamworks.

FUTURE FINANCES

Paul is saving for the future. He's decided to make a game out of it. Match the deposits to the correct cubbyhole.

2 x $3.00

$7 + $3.00

2 x $2.00

$6.00 + 50 cents

3 x $3.00

half a dollar

90 cents + 9 cents

2 x $1.00

99 cents

$6.00

$6.50

$4.00

$10.00

50 cents

$9.00

$2.00

Many Monies
Money has taken many forms throughout history, from metals to shells to paper. The one thing they all have in common is they have to be relatively rare or difficult to make.

Money Doesn't Grow on Trees!

Ever heard that expression? It came into being because in China coins used to be attached to metal that looked like branches and had to be broken off to be used. What do you think this expression means today?

STOCKS FOR YOU!

Decide if the stocks you've investigated would be good choices for you. Which is the best choice? Use the last sale price to figure out how many shares you could buy with $1,000. You've begun the investing game. Set a date in the future, perhaps six months, when you will finish tracking your stock. Over the six months, look at the stock listings. You don't have to do this every day; once a week would be good. You might want to graph your stock's price on a weekly basis.

At the six-month point, take the close price that day and multiply it by the number of shares you bought with your original $1,000. How did you do? Did you make money? If so, what is the percentage of increase? (Divide the present value of your stock by the amount you started with: $1,000. For example, your stock is now worth $1,150. If you divide 1,150 by 1,000, you will get 1.15. That means you earned a 15 percent increase!)

If you feel comfortable with the results of your investing game, then perhaps you'd like to ask your parents if you could try investing with real money. By law, you are not able to invest on your own if you are not of legal age. The definition of legal age varies from state to state. Your parents would have to set up a custodial or guardian account for you. Or maybe your parents invest in the stock market themselves and they could show you how some of their investments have done and what they use to help them make decisions.

Real Money Investing

How do you go about investing with real money? You could find a broker, someone who does the buying and selling for you. There are basically two types of brokers. A full-service broker trades stocks for you and also provides you with investment advice. A discount broker merely buys and sells the stock that you tell him to. The advantage to the discount broker is that the fees for the service are less than for a full-service broker. People who want to buy stocks can also use companies like ING Direct and E-Trade to buy stocks at a low fee. If you are new to investing or can't take the time to do your own research, then it may be worth it to pay the extra money for the advice of a professional. It is also possible to buy some individual shares of stock directly from the companies.

If your parents or relatives want to purchase stock for you, let them know about the Uniform Gift to Minors Act (UGMA) and the Uniform Transfer to Minors Act (UTMA). These laws allow adults to have control over the gifts or transfers of money, stock, real estate, and so on, to children under legal age, or in the case of UTMA, children up to twenty-five years of age. There are tax advantages to setting up this kind of account. To find out more, your parents can order IRS publication 929, "Tax Rules for Children and Dependents," by calling 1-800-TAX-FORM or visiting *www.irs.gov*.

Dollars & Sense

Don't Put All Your Eggs in One Basket

If you get excited about one stock or one company, it is tempting to invest all your money there. But if that company doesn't do well, you won't make any money. A wise investor invests in a wide variety of companies.

MUTUAL FUND MOOLAH

Mutual fund investing is perfect for the investor who has neither the time nor the desire to research individual companies, wants diversification, and doesn't have a lot of money.

What is a mutual fund? A mutual fund is a group of people (investors) pooling their money to invest in a group of stocks, bonds, and other securities (another word for stocks and bonds).

A mutual fund is controlled by a person known as a fund manager. The fund manager, through her knowledge and experience, selects a number of different securities for the fund. Mutual funds are available through brokerage houses and investment companies.

Mutual funds come in the following varieties:

WORDS to KNOW

DIVERSIFICATION: Diversification is to invest money in a wide variety of companies or industries.

- **Stock funds** own stock in companies. Like stocks, mutual funds can be defined as growth or income investments.

- **Bond funds** own a number of different bonds or specialize in one type of bond.
- **Money market funds** own short-term investments such as CDs.
- **Balanced funds** own both stocks and bonds.
- **A real estate investment trust (REIT)** buys real estate (buildings and land).
- **Other funds** invest in gold or foreign stocks and bonds.

Diversification and professional management are the main advantages to mutual funds. For instance, a stock fund will invest in the stocks of a variety of different industries. Over a period of time, some stock may go down, others may go up. Hopefully, the fund has more ups so that the total value of your investment grows over time! Some mutual funds allow you to invest with smaller amounts of money than would be required by a brokerage house (company that trades stocks and bonds) for investing in stocks. There are even some plans where you can invest a fixed amount each month.

The disadvantage to mutual funds is that the return on your investment may not be as high as the return on the stock market. Remember the 9.5 percent average yearly return on stocks? Typically, a mutual fund does not earn as much, with average yearly earnings of about 8%.

How to Understand Mutual Funds

Funds offer an investor a prospectus. A prospectus is a written statement of the fund's objectives—what it hopes to do. It also tells you the fund's performance history, its fees, its special features, the minimum required to invest in the fund, and the level of risk. For example, growth stock mutual funds are riskier than income stock funds. Before investing in any mutual fund, you should read the prospectus carefully. You can also do a little research by looking at the *Morningstar Mutual Funds*, a weekly rating of mutual funds, or visiting *www.morningstar.com*.

Like the stock market, mutual funds are listed online. Just like stocks, listings vary from website to website, but here is what you will usually find:

- **Net asset value.** This is the dollar value of one share of the fund. If you were to sell the share back to the company, this is the price you would get.
- **Trade time.** This was when the most recent trade was made.
- **Change.** This shows both the amount and the percent of change.
- **Previous close.** This was the price of the mutual fund at the close of the previous business day.
- **YTD return.** This is the percentage change for the year from January 1 through today.
- **Net assets.** This is the total amount of money the mutual fund is worth.
- **Yield.** This is the dividend divided by the price per share, and it shows what percentage of your investment you will receive in dividends.

This is only a beginning look at the investment opportunities kids can look forward to. If you are interested in finding out more, you're in luck. There are hundreds of books about investing! Just go to your local library or bookstore and prepare to be overwhelmed by the amount of information.

INVEST IN YOURSELF

Instead of investing your money in the stock market, you might consider investing money in your college education.

Fun Facts

Buy a Share

You can buy one share of stock of a company you like, such as Disney or Starbucks, at *www.oneshare.com*. You need an adult to make the purchase for you.

Bulls and Bears

You may have heard the stock market referred to as a bull or bear market. No, there aren't animals on Wall Street! A *bull market* occurs when stock prices rise. A *bear market* is when stock prices go down.

$

Dollars & Sense

Luck of the Draw

Some adults buy lottery tickets thinking it is an investment. The problem is that you are guaranteed nothing, and the odds of winning anything are quite small. It's not a real investment at all. Buying a lottery ticket once in a while can be a fun game of chance, but it's not a sound way to earn money.

College probably seems like a long way off, but the money you save today could help you pay tuition, buy books, or pay other education costs. Your parents can open a special account called a 529 plan. The money you invest in the account can only be used for education. The plan is like a mutual fund in a way. The plan managers invest plan money in the stock market, and that money placed in the account grows, just like it does if you put money in a mutual fund. The good news is that the money earned in a 529 plan is not taxed!

You, your parents, and other relatives can invest money in your account. When you're ready for college, this money will be waiting to help pay for it! A 529 plan is an investment in yourself because the money you spend on college will be repaid when you get a good job after you get your degree.

OWN THE GOVERNMENT!

If you want to invest but you're nervous about the risks of the stock market, you might want to think about buying government bonds. This is like buying stock in the government. The best part about it is that it's a risk-free investment. The government guarantees a certain rate of return on the money you invest. You don't have to worry about the government going out of business or being unable to pay its investors.

You pay the government to buy a bond, and the government uses the money to help run the country. Individual investors can buy savings bonds, so this is the best way to invest in the government. Fifty million Americans own savings bonds, totaling over $200 billion dollars. That's a lot of cash!

Series EE bonds are one of the most common types. You buy the bond at half off the face value. When you cash the bond in at maturity (the number of years it is meant to last), you get the full face value. If you buy a Series EE bond that has a face value of $100, you spend only $50 to buy it. If your bond matures in eight years and you cash it in then, you will get $100. If you wait past the maturity date, you will get the face value plus additional money that it has earned.

COOL COLLECTIBLES

Do you collect Pokémon cards? Or maybe on your shelf in your room you keep a couple of metal lunchboxes your dad had as a kid. Surely you've seen a baseball card! These are collectibles. Collectibles are things that have value to collectors. A collection of dust bunnies from under your bed wouldn't be considered collectibles, but a collection of comic books would.

Collectibles are an investment opportunity. Everyone dreams about finding an old coin that is worth thousands of dollars! Unfortunately, the risk involved does not make collectibles investment a good choice for kids. You need to be very well educated to know what is a good buy. But collecting can be fun, and won't it be great if your collection increases in value over the years?

If your collection has potential value, it is important for you to learn all you can about the collection and how to care for it. Most collectibles are valuable because they are in perfect or near-perfect condition. They are worth less if they are scuffed up or broken. If you have a Star Wars action figure collection and all the action figures are unopened in their original boxes, they are worth much more than action figures you've played with. That's the hard part about collectibles—if they are going to have value they are really just for looking at, not playing with. Collectibles are also more valuable as a set. If you have a collection of every Barbie doll issued in a certain year, that has more value than if you just have a few of them.

Collectibles that are hard to find are worth more. A baseball signed by Babe Ruth is valuable because there are only a certain number of those available.

TRY THIS

Collection Investigation
No matter what kind of collection you or your parents have, there is probably a book or website that will help you determine its value. Do some research and find out how much your collections are really worth right now.

QUIRKY COLLECTOR

This quirky collector has a secret hideaway for her collection of rare coins. She has some very unique character traits, but luckily they will help lead us to the hiding place. Let's go!

She doesn't like heights.

She doesn't like sports.

She is a vegetarian.

She's afraid of plaid.

She burns easily in the sun.

She loves animals.

She likes to stay south of the beach.

Nice Numismatic
Coin collecting is known as the hobby of kings and even has its very own name: numismatics.

A collection of Monopoly game pieces is less valuable since there are thousands of them. The most important thing is that you are interested in your collection and have fun adding to it and taking care of it.

VIRTUAL DOLLARS ARE VIRTUAL FUN!

While real money is a lot of fun to use and earn more money with, you can also earn virtual money. You can earn points online so that you can buy things on certain websites.

Webkinz are an exciting way to use virtual dollars. A Webkinz is a stuffed animal you can buy or ask for as a gift. The animal comes with a code that you register at the Webkinz website, *www.webkinz.com*. You get to choose a name for your pet and decide if it is a boy or girl. The site gives you some Kidzcash to start—these are your virtual dollars. Your pet gets its own room and you use the virtual money to buy things for the room, as well as food and supplies for your pet. The site tracks how well you care for your pet.

You can earn more virtual dollars by playing games and taking quizzes. The more virtual dollars you earn, the more cool stuff you can "buy" on the site for your pet's room. The site also lets you invite friends to play in your virtual room with their pets. Use your dollars wisely! If you run out, you won't be able to buy food for your pet!

There are lots of other websites where you can earn and use virtual dollars like *www.clubpenguin.com* (where you own a cute penguin) and *www.nicktropolis.com* (which allows you to access great Nickelodeon character items). When using virtual spending sites, there are a few things to be careful about:

- If they ask for you to get parental permission, make sure you do it. Your parents want to know what you're doing online and want to be sure you are on safe sites.

Dollars & Sense

Collectible Joy
If keeping your collection in mint (unused) condition just makes you miserable because you want to play with it or use it, it might be time to think of another collection to start. It can be hard to collect toys because, really, the whole purpose of toys is to play with them!

- Some sites require you to pay real money to get advanced memberships where you can do more. Talk about this with your parents and think about whether you will play on the site enough to make it worth the money.
- If the site has a chat room where you can talk to other players, never give out your real name, address, or phone number. Most sites run programs that block you from posting this information, but you still need to be careful. Never agree to meet someone you meet online. Always tell your parents if someone says something scary or weird to you.
- Don't lose yourself online. It can be easy to spend all of your time on these sites, playing with your characters and earning virtual dollars. Make sure you do other things—play outside, read, do homework, and do things with your family.

Virtual money is sometimes better than real money because you don't have to worry so much when you spend it!

The EVERYTHING KIDS' Money Book

Chapter 7
WHAT STUFF COSTS

FUN ISN'T FREE

Money truly does make the world go around. In order to buy anything or have anyone do any kind of service or work, you have to pay for it. Nobody works for free, so anything a person creates, fixes, or does costs money. It would be great if you could go to the store and pick out a DVD for free, but the actors who are in the movie have to be paid, the people who filmed the movie need to be paid, and the people who actually produced the disc and case also have to be paid for their time and the cost of the materials. Every time you buy something, you are helping to pay the salaries of the people who helped create the thing or service you are buying.

You may not realize it, but almost everything you use or do every day costs money. Let's look at a typical day for you.

- **Morning.** You wake up in your bed in your pajamas. You run water to brush your teeth. You pour cereal in a bowl. You put on clothes and shoes. Every part of this costs money—the bed, water, toothpaste, cereal, bowl, clothes, and shoes.

- **School.** You ride the bus to school. You sit at your desk and use a pencil to do a worksheet. The teacher talks to the class. You have lunch in the cafeteria and then go to art class where you paint a picture. You ride the bus home. Again, it all costs money—the bus and the school itself cost money to build. Your teacher gets paid a salary. Your lunch had to be paid for, and someone had to buy the paint, the pencil, and the worksheet.

- **Afternoon.** You come home and watch television, have a snack, and then play a game with your brother. You put on your rollerblades and skate outside. Your parents make dinner and you sit at the table and eat together. You guessed it—everything from the television and the snack to the game and your rollerblades costs money. Even the sidewalks you skated on cost money! The food you ate and the table you ate at all had to be purchased somewhere!

The EVERYTHING KIDS' Money Book

- **Evening.** It gets dark, so your parents turn on the lights. You take a bath and then do a puzzle. Your mom shows you a game on the computer. Your parents pay for the electricity, the puzzle, the Internet access, and the computer. All of it costs money.

It seems like the world is made of money if you think about it closely, doesn't it? There are actually a couple of different ways that the costs of things are paid for.

Public Costs

There are many things in your life that you or your parents don't directly pay for, but you still contribute to them whether you realize it or not. If you go to a public school, your parents don't have to pay in order for you to go there. Anyone who lives in your neighborhood can go to the school without having to pay. However, schools are expensive—the buildings, supplies, furniture, heat, lights, water, and teachers' salaries are all big costs.

SPLASH MONEY

Summer is coming and Carla is getting things for the beach. But she can't decide which store has a better deal. Can you help?

PayLittle
Swimsuit	$12.00
Flippers	$4.00
Mask	$3.00
Water wings	$2.50

BuyMore
Swimsuit	$9.00
Flippers	$5.00
Mask	$6.00
Water wings	$2.00

SpendLess
Swimsuit	$6.00
Flippers	$6.50
Mask	$7.00
Water wings	$3.00

ADD UP DINNER

Allen wants to go out for dinner. He has $7.00. Is that enough to get what he's thinking about?

Hamburger $4.00

Milkshake $2.00

Fries $1.00

Flip and Spin

Did you know that you can do cartwheels with your fingers or hold a Ferris wheel in your hand? Both are nicknames for a silver dollar!

Things like schools are paid for by the government. It's not a freebie for everyone, though! People pay taxes and the government uses some of that money to run schools. Tax money is also used to build sidewalks, run hospitals, pay firefighters, and mow the grass in the park.

What's interesting is that everyone must contribute to these costs, but even though your parents have to pay a school tax, they can't make decisions about what happens at the school. In our system of government, the people we elect to run our government are the ones who decide how to use the money we pay in taxes. This is one reason why it is important to vote—so that you can have a say in who is going to spend your money!

WORDS to KNOW

BENEFITS: A benefit is something an employee receives as part of his or her job that has a money value. Health insurance is one common benefit, but your dad's employer might also pay for his cell phone if he uses it for work.

Private Costs

Many things that cost money are paid for by individuals. Your parents pay for food, furniture, and your ticket to the movies (unless you pay for that yourself!). Your family may also have some things that are paid for directly by one of your parents' employers. Many companies pay for their employees' health insurance, and they might also provide a car or other items for the employee to use.

The places where you buy things also pay costs themselves. When you go to a restaurant, the owner of the restaurant has to buy all the food, plates, silverware, and furniture, and she must also pay the waiters, cooks, and busboys who work there. The owner also has to pay rent, electricity, and water bills to keep the actual restaurant building open. The store you buy a pack of gum at must buy the gum from the company that makes it and pay the person who delivers it to the store, as well as pay all the people who work in the store.

DOLLARS FOR DINNER

Americans spend about $341 a week on food for their families. That might not seem like a lot, but compare it to the costs in other countries:

Pizza Garden

If you and your family want to save some cash on pizza, how about planting one? You can't grow an actual pizza, but you can grow the ingredients. Mark out a circle of open ground, divide it into slices, and plant tomatoes, basil, oregano, pepper, and any other veggies you like on your pizza in the slices. When your veggies are grown, you can use them to make homemade pizza and save the money it would cost to have one delivered!

WORDS to KNOW

ORGANIC: Organic food is food grown without pesticides.

- Bhutan $5
- Chad $1
- China $155
- Ecuador $31
- Egypt $68
- Great Britain $253
- Italy $260
- Japan $317
- Mexico $189
- Mongolia $40
- Poland $155

Where and how you get your food affects the cost. If your family goes out to dinner at a pizza place, your parents are likely to spend at least $40. If you stayed home and made your own pizza and salad, the ingredients would likely only cost about $10. If your family grew its own vegetables and made its own dough, the cost would be even less – only a few dollars. Why the difference? The more people that are involved with your food—growing it, picking it, canning it, shipping it, selling it, cooking it, serving it—the more cost is involved.

Another thing that affects the cost of your family's food is the type of food you buy. You know that if you go to Francoise's FrouFrou Café and get lobster and steak you will pay a lot more than if you go to McDonald's and get a Happy Meal. Another difference is the type of food your family picks out at the supermarket. A lot of families are buying organic food because it is healthier for you. However, organic food costs more because farmers have to spend more time caring for the food or livestock.

PETS EAT, TOO!

If you have a pet, that furry little fella is probably a lot of fun for you and your whole family. But pet food doesn't grow on trees, you know! Pets can actually be pretty expensive. If your family buys a puppy from a breeder, you could spend hundreds of dollars. It usually costs less to adopt a pet from an animal rescue organization, but you will still have to make a donation.

If you've got a pet, you've got to take care of it. You need food, vet visits, and things like litter boxes, cages, toys, or tanks to keep your pet happy and healthy. All of these items can add up to big bucks.

If you are thinking about getting a pet, it can be helpful to understand how much it will really cost to take care of your new pal. Check out the SPCA (Society for the Prevention of Cruelty to Animals) website, which shows yearly budgets for different types of pets: *www. spca.bc.ca/AnimalCare/petcost.asp*. You might be surprised to find out that a dog costs more than $1,000 a year!

BRAIN POWER: SCHOOL COSTS

Public schools are paid for by school taxes, which are paid by people who own property in the community your school is in. If you go to a private school, your parents must pay tuition for you to attend. The average cost of private school tuition is $12,500 a year. Even if you go to a public school, your education isn't free. The average family spends about $500 on school supplies every year.

Thinking about college? It can be a big expense. But, just like school now, it depends on what kind of college you go to. Public colleges are run by the state and cost much less than private colleges which require students and their families to pay higher tuition. Right now the average cost of a private college is $23,700 a year. A public college averages $12,300 a year. College costs go up every year. Sounds like a lot of money, right? Maybe, but the U.S. Census Bureau says that a college degree can increase your lifetime income by $2 million. Sounds worth it for sure, wouldn't you say?

Chapter 7: What Stuff Costs

PENNY FOR YOUR THOUGHTS

Rising Costs

In 1920, a loaf of bread cost 10 cents and a gallon of milk cost 28 cents. Today, bread is $2 and milk is $3.72. Why do you think the costs are so different? How are prices related to the value of the dollar?

WORDS to KNOW

TUITION: Tuition is a fee paid to attend a school.

Fun Fact

Turkey Talk

The average cost of the Thanksgiving dinner (including pumpkin pie!) for a family gathering of ten people is $42. That's a lot of turkey!

$

Dollars & Sense

Although college does cost a lot, there are a lot of ways to make it more affordable. Many students get scholarships—money given to them by the school or other organizations as a reward for good grades. Lots of students borrow money from banks to pay for their college educations. See Chapter 4 to learn about 529 plans, special college savings plans you can start right now to help you and your family pay for college!

CLOTHES AND SHOES

A study showed that it costs about $50 a month to buy clothes and shoes for kids your age. The older you get, the more expensive your clothes are. Clothing is one type of item that is sold with a wide range of prices. You can shop at a discount store and buy things for very inexpensive prices, or you can shop for big name brands at high-end stores and spend much more.

Another factor that affects the cost of clothes and shoes is how they are made. The less the company has to pay the workers who make the clothes, the more profit they can make. The United Nations is very concerned about clothes that are made in foreign countries by children. There are children in foreign countries who work hours and hours each day for pennies. Child labor is a common problem in the clothing industry and many companies are taking steps to be sure the clothes they sell are not made by children.

HOME SWEET HOME

If your family owns the home you live in, you've probably never thought about how much the house really cost. The average cost of a house in the United States is $264,000. Sounds like a lot of dough to come up with, doesn't it? Most people don't pay cash for their homes, though. Most families get a mortgage. A mortgage is a special loan that you can get from a bank in order to

Baffling Banks

Julie is going to the bank to pay her mortgage, but she's having trouble getting there. Cross out the words described below, then read the message that's left to see which is the correct bank. When you find the correct path, add up the numbers alongside to see how much Julie's mortgage is.

Words with DD in them

Words that end in Y

Words that rhyme with CLUE

Words that begin with GR

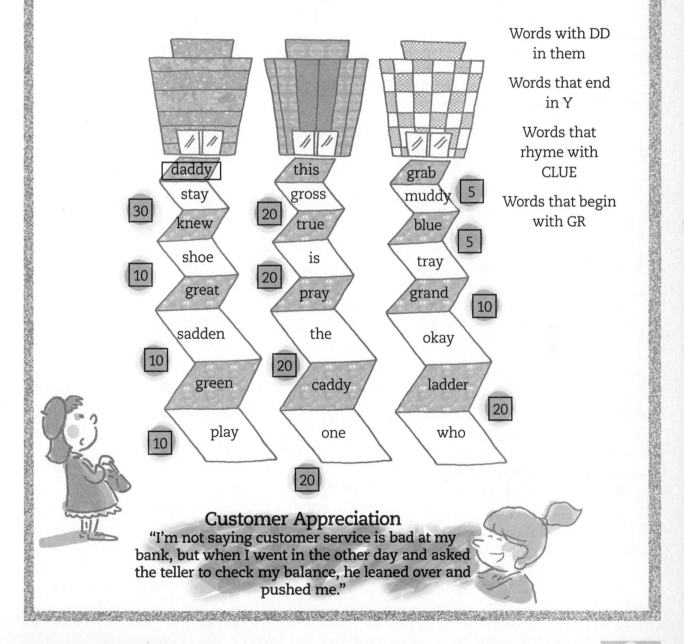

Bank 1	Bank 2	Bank 3
daddy	this	grab
stay	gross	muddy — 5
30 — knew	20 — true	blue — 5
shoe	is	tray
10 — great	20 — pray	grand — 10
sadden	the	okay
10 — green	20 — caddy	ladder — 20
play	one	who
10	20	

Customer Appreciation

"I'm not saying customer service is bad at my bank, but when I went in the other day and asked the teller to check my balance, he leaned over and pushed me."

Dollars & Sense

Carpooling

Carpooling is another way to save on transportation costs. If you and your friend are both going to the library, instead of two parents driving two cars and using gas, one parent could drive you both and cut the cost in half. Plus, it's more fun to do things with friends!

buy a home. The homebuyer has to provide a down payment (an amount of cash) to show that he can invest in the home. The bank provides the rest of the cash payment to the person selling the home. The new homeowner then has to pay the bank a certain amount of money every month for a number of years (often 30 years) until the loan is completely paid back. The average monthly mortgage payment is $1,300, according to the U.S. Census. The bank earns interest on the amount it lent and the homeowner gets the benefit of living in a house he could not afford to buy any other way.

Families who do not own the house or apartment they live in pay rent, which is a monthly payment to the owner of the building to pay for the right to live there. How much does it cost to rent? About $700 a month on average, according to the U.S. Census Bureau.

GETTING AROUND

If you take buses or subways, you are used to paying for your rides. Public transportation like this is more common in large cities. In some cities, buses and subways are paid for with tokens; small pieces of metal that look like coins but are not legal tender anywhere except on the bus or subway. Tokens were made in a variety of shapes, sizes, and colors for different cities and are now collector's items. Most transportation systems now use cards that look like credit cards. You buy one from a worker or a vending machine and can put any amount of money on it you want. You swipe the card through a reader to get on the bus or subway. Each time you ride, the cost of the ride is deducted from the card.

Public transportation is a way for a large group of people to share transportation costs. Instead of all 30 people driving their own cars to work, they all get on one bus and split the cost. Public transportation also helps reduce pollution. Taxis are another common type of transportation in a city, where you pay the driver a fare for the cost of the ride.

Many families own cars, trucks, or vans which they use to go places. People who own cars have to buy them, sometimes taking out a loan to do so. You can also rent or lease a car for a few days or a few years. Cars need gas to run and gas prices have gone up drastically in recent years. Cars also need repairs, registrations (a permit from the state to use the car), and upkeep, all of which cost money.

There are some types of transportation that are practically free, though. Walking will take you places. So will riding a bike, scooter, or skateboard or rollerblading. They're cheap and fun, and the exercise is great for your body!

PAY TO PLAY

OK, so you totally get it, not much is free. Have you ever thought about how much all the fun little things cost, though? Check out this list of today's average costs:

- Movie ticket $6.55
- DVD rental $4
- Candy bar $1
- Paperback children's book $4.95
- Ski lift ticket $60
- Playstation game $40
- Barbie doll $15
- Computer $1000
- iPod $115

That's a lot of moolah for fun, isn't it?

When you think about how much you or your family spends on fun, though, it's important to think about how you use the item. A game that your family plays over and over is money well spent. A computer you use to do homework is an important tool, and once you're finished you can play games or use the Internet.

PENNY FOR YOUR THOUGHTS

Free Fun

How many fun things can you think of to do that don't cost a cent? Make a list and see how many you can come up with! Your parents and grandparents might have some great ideas of things they did when they were kids that are free, too. Ask them and see what they suggest.

Chapter 8
SUPER SPENDING

Savings for a new bike

Dollars & Sense

How Do You Spend?

Do you know where all of your money goes? Take a month and write down every single thing you spend money on. At the end of the month, you will be able to see exactly how you have been using your money. Consider whether you're spending it or using it in the wisest ways.

THINK IT OVER: NEEDS AND WANTS

In Chapter 7, you learned a lot about how much things cost. You can only buy something if you have enough money for it. Part of learning to be responsible with money is learning how to manage your money so that you spend wisely, buy things you really need, and plan out how you are going to handle your money. Making these choices can be tough.

It is easy to mix up what you need with what you want. Sometimes you want something so badly that you feel like you need it and have to have it. All your friends might have the latest gadget and you feel like you have to have it, too. Or you see a cool shirt in a store window and you can't think about anything else but finding the money to afford it.

There is a big difference between needs and wants, though. A need is something you cannot manage without. You need food, shelter, education, and clothes. No matter what, you've got to have those things to survive and keep your life moving forward. If you think about the lives of kids in less fortunate countries, you realize that much of what we have is unnecessary in these basic terms.

A want is something that you would like to have, but it's not the end of the world if you don't get it. There are a lot of wants that are definitely important, however. You want a new notebook for school, or you want a new hair gel. These are things that you will use every day.

The hard thing is understanding what is a want and what is a need, and then taking the wants and ranking them in order of importance. No matter how big your allowance is, there's no way you can afford all of your wants all at once!

Bikes and Barbie Houses: Big Splurges

There may be big items you would like but can't afford to buy right now. Whether you want a bike, electronic game system, Barbie house, giant Lego set, iPod, or something else, it can be frustrating to want something desperately but not have the cash to make the purchase! The best way to afford a big item is to investigate the cost. Find out exactly how much money you need. Talk to your parents. Sometimes parents are willing to match what you save toward a large purchase so that you only actually have to save half of the price from your own dollars.

Once you know how much it's going to cost, think about how much money you can save per week. Can you put aside part of your weekly allowance? Could you pick up a few extra babysitting or lawn raking jobs to make some extra cash? Do you have a birthday or holiday coming up where relatives will give you money? Once you figure out how much money you've got available, you can set up a savings plan. If you can save or earn $10 a week and the item you want costs $100, you know it will take you 10 weeks to get enough money for the big buy. Don't forget that you will probably have to pay sales tax on your item, so be sure to add that into the total purchase price.

Once you've reached your savings goal, you really have something to be proud of. Making that big purchase is a special moment, and one that you have worked hard to earn. Ask your parents to take a picture of you with your new buy so that you can remember the victory of this great moment!

Figure It Out: Budgeting Basics

Once you have money to control, you need to start to think about what you want that money to be for. Do you

Fun Fact

Change Adds Up

According to one study, people lose more than $58 million each year just in change they drop into airline seats. Next time you're on a plane, check for some loose change in your seat!

TRY THIS

Break a Habit

If you or someone in your family is trying to break a bad habit (like chewing your nails or forgetting to turn off the bathroom light), set up a special payment jar. Each time you or someone else goofs and does the thing they're trying to stop, that person has to put a certain amount of money in the jar (a dime, a quarter, or whatever you agree on). Your family can then use the money for something fun for everyone.

want to be able to spend whatever you have spontaneously whenever the mood strikes you? Do you want to save your money and spend as little as possible? Or do you want to be able to do both? Some people are definitely more comfortable with one method or the other, but many kids find that they can save some money and spend some money.

It can be hard to decide how to spend (or save) your money. One day you might feel like doing one thing, while another day you might want to do something else. And you might have those times when you desperately need money for something (like a school lunch or a birthday gift for your mom) but are totally broke and unprepared.

If you take some time to think about your money and spending, you can make sure you always have enough moolah on hand for what you need. The best way to do this is to create a budget. First, think about expenses you have that don't happen every week—like your mom's

BUDGET BETH

Beth is on a budget. She has $84 and it has to last twelve weeks. Can you budget how much she can spend each week? The cumulative totals for each week are listed below—but there are three missing! Can you figure out the totals for each of the three missing weeks?

$77	$28	$35
$49	$63	$84
$14	$7	$70

birthday gift, souvenirs on vacation, holiday gift costs, or new earrings. Don't forget about things like gifts for your friends' birthday parties. You should think about the whole year so that you remember everyone's birthday and every event. Enter these items into Table 8-1.

Table 8-1
Irregular Expenses

Type of Expense	Amount
Total:	

Now that you know how much you need to spend on these kinds of expenses, take your total from the last row in Table 8-1 and divide it by 52. This is how much money you need to save every week in order to have money to pay for all of these expenses.

Now let's take a look at what your weekly expenses look like. Think about the things you need to have money for every week. This could be for school lunch, entry to a skateboard park with friends, or a pack of gum. Don't forget to list the amount of money you want to put away in a savings account each week. Use the

Dollars & Sense

Budget Sense
A budget might seem sort of hard to deal with, but remember, you're in charge of your money. If you find you need to spend some extra money this week for something unexpected, it's OK! You can spend less in the coming weeks to make up for it.

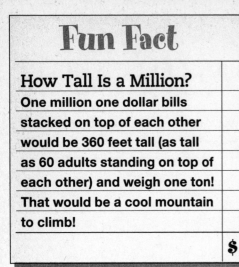
tables below to help you figure out what your weekly budget should look like.

Table 8-2

Weekly Expenses

Item	Amount

Weekly Amount for Irregular Expenses
(the number you got by dividing the
total of Table 8-1 by 52) _____

Total _____

Now you can see how much money you need each week to pay for your regular expenses and to set money aside for your special occasion expenses. If you don't earn enough money each week to cover these costs, remember that you will probably get some gifts of money throughout the year that you can add to your savings. You can also think about ways to earn more money. Another choice is to take a look at your expenses and find ways to cut them back. Maybe you could pack a lunch instead of buying one at school. Instead of going

HOW MUCH IS IT?

If you want to buy things, it sure helps if you're good with numbers.
Can you figure out which equation doesn't fit in each price tag?

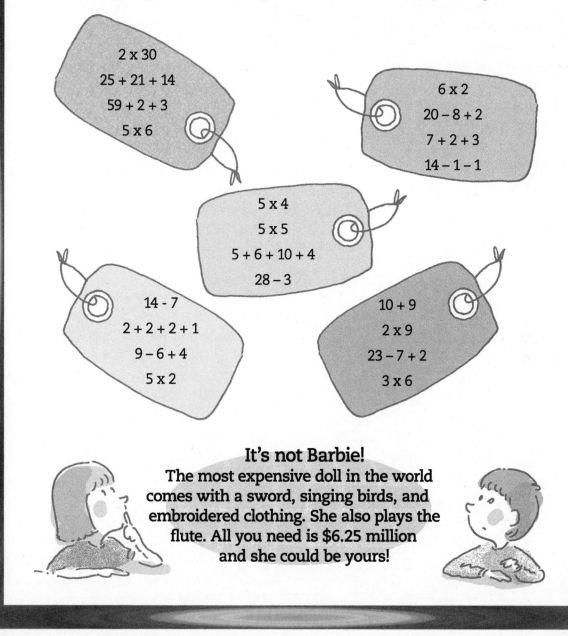

2 x 30
25 + 21 + 14
59 + 2 + 3
5 x 6

6 x 2
20 − 8 + 2
7 + 2 + 3
14 − 1 − 1

5 x 4
5 x 5
5 + 6 + 10 + 4
28 − 3

14 - 7
2 + 2 + 2 + 1
9 − 6 + 4
5 x 2

10 + 9
2 x 9
23 − 7 + 2
3 x 6

It's not Barbie!

The most expensive doll in the world comes with a sword, singing birds, and embroidered clothing. She also plays the flute. All you need is $6.25 million and she could be yours!

PENNY FOR YOUR THOUGHTS

Sale Sense

Why do you think stores have sales? Do you think they make a profit on items they have on sale? Do you think that people who come in to shop the sales also buy other things while they are there?

to the movies with your friends each week, maybe you can only afford to go every other week.

SMART SHOPPING

When you do decide to spend your money, you want to make sure you get the best price. You don't want to spend $15 for a CD if you could have gotten it at another store for $12. There are lots of great ways to save money and be a smart shopper—if you know what to look for.

Comparison Shopping

Comparison shopping means you compare prices at different stores before you make a purchase. You don't have to get your parents to drive you to every store in the universe, though. You can do a lot of your comparison shopping online. Most large stores have websites where you can check the price of an item.

Sale Shopping

If your family gets a newspaper, you might already know that every Sunday the paper comes with a huge pile of ads from local stores. If you know you want to buy a certain DVD, you can check the sale ads to see if it is on sale anywhere. Sometimes stores print coupons in their ads that save you money on purchases as well. It's also important to know that if you buy something and the store puts it on sale the next week, you can usually go back and get the difference between what you paid and what the sale price is.

Earn Points

If there is a store you shop at a lot, ask if they have a shopper's card or a discount card. Many stores have special cards that give you extra discounts or earn you points toward a free purchase when you use them. You may also receive special coupons or offers in the mail. The store may require that only adults can have cards. If that's the case, ask your parents to sign up for one for you.

Bargain Hunting

There are lots of great ways to save money on things you want to buy. Try some of these ideas:

- **Second hand stores.** Second hand or thrift stores are a great place to find incredible buys and unusual items you can't find anywhere else.
- **Clearance rack.** Most stores have a clearance rack or discounted section with items they have marked down to sell quickly. You can save half of the regular selling price or more by checking this section of the store.
- **Yard sales.** People sell things they no longer want at yard sales, tag sales, or garage sales. Lots of times people whose children are grown want to get rid of toys, games, books, and other kid's items and are willing to sell them for pennies. Check out the yard sales in your neighborhood to see what's for sale!
- **eBay.** Your parents can help you look for great prices on things on eBay.com, a website that is like a big garage sale. People list items they want to sell. If you're interested, your parents can bid on items. The person with the highest bid wins!

Impulse Shopping

Avoid buying on impulse when possible. Stores are designed to convince you to buy things. They don't really want you to take the time to think things over. It can be really tempting to snap up a T-shirt or a cool set of gel pens. You can spend a lot of money on these kinds of purchases if you aren't careful.

The better plan is to go home and think about it. Consider how much it costs and how big a bite that would take out of your weekly budget or your savings.

Disappearing Dollar
Get ready for this trick by taking out two dollars. Fold one over two-thirds of the way across. Place the other bill over the crease of the fold, hiding the fold from view. To start the trick, show your money to the audience; it will look like three bills. Tell them you are going to make one disappear. Hold the bottom edges of the bill between your thumb and first finger. Shake it so the bill unfolds. Poof! You've turned three bills into only two!

Fun Fact

Science of Shopping
Did you know there are people who study shopping? They research what colors make people want to buy, where to put things on shelves, how stores should smell, and which direction people turn when they first walk into a shop. The stores you go to are carefully arranged in order to get you to buy more, more, more!

DARE TO COMPARE

Trying to get the best value for your money can be confusing. You will find the best deal if you keep an eagle eye on prices and compare. Which one of these is the cheapest?

$65.00 + $7.00 tax

No tax today!

$35.00 each

$110.00 with a $30.00 Rebate

Think about other things you might want to buy or things you are saving for. Weigh these things in your mind against the cool thing you just saw in the store. You might still decide you want to buy it—and that's OK! Once you've thought it over, you know it's something you really want and something that is worth that amount of money to you. You might also decide that you don't really want it, or you may not want to pay that much for that type of item. That's OK, too! Making these kinds of choices makes you a smart shopper!

WORDS to KNOW

IMPULSE BUY: Purchasing something on the spur of the moment without thinking it through and making an educated decision is called making an impulse buy.

The EVERYTHING KIDS' Money Book

Chapter 9

SHARE THE WEALTH

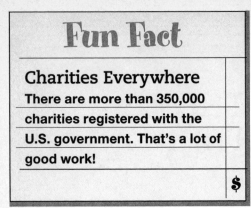

WORDS to KNOW

NONPROFIT AGENCY: A nonprofit agency is a charity that works to help people or a cause and does not earn any money itself.

WHAT IS A CHARITY?

As long as there have been humans, they have helped each other. It was the only way that a group of people could survive. As humans evolved and created civilizations, they continued to rely on each other. In the Middle Ages, people in Europe were required to tithe, or pay 10% of their income to the Catholic church. The church used some of that money to help people who needed assistance. People don't have to tithe anymore, but they continued to believe that they should give to each other.

Today, a charity is an organization that is dedicated to helping other people. Most people do things to help other people. Your mom might drive your elderly neighbor to the grocery store, or you might lend your friend a pencil to take the math test with. These are wonderful things to do, but they are not the same as the organized work a charity does.

A charity is an organization whose only purpose is to help people or support a cause. It might provide medical care to sick kids, offer scholarships, assist people in finding jobs, rescue injured wildlife, or do other needed things. In order to do that important work, it needs to collect or raise money or goods. Some charities look like big companies, but the difference is that a charity does not make a profit for itself. The people who are employed by the charity are paid to do their jobs, but the company as a whole does not earn a profit.

For example, the Red Cross is a huge charity. It helps people who are homeless because of natural disasters (like hurricanes), and it also collects blood which is donated to people in hospitals who need it. There are thousands of people who work for the Red Cross and are paid for their work. However, the Red Cross itself does not earn a profit. Its goal is to help other people, not to make money for itself.

Charities don't have to pay taxes. To get this special tax-free status, they must first offer proof to the government that they are actually a charity. Charities that

BOXED SURPRISES

These kids are all donating gifts to people they don't know, but they've been told what their new friends enjoy doing. Match each gift with the correct person!

BIG Billions

In 2006, billionaire Warren Buffett donated $37 billion to the Bill and Melinda Gates Foundation, one of the largest charities in the world. Buffett's donation is the largest charitable gift ever made in the United States.

ADMINISTRATIVE COSTS: Administrative costs are the money a charity spends on running its business instead of directly helping people or its cause. These can include things like paying salaries and benefits for the people who work for the charity, buying new computers and office supplies, and replacing the hot water heater in the office.

meet the test are called 501(c)(3) charities. This means that the U.S. government agrees that they are true charities that do not have to pay taxes. When you are evaluating a charity it's a good idea to be sure it is actually an official 501(c)(3) charity. Anyone can claim to be a charity, but only real ones get the tax designation.

WHO CAN I HELP?

The great thing about charities is that there are so many of them. Because of this, it is easy to find one that interests you. There are charities for specific diseases and medical conditions; these organizations pay for research that might find cures and treatments. If someone in your family has a disease or medical condition, there is likely a charity for it.

There are also charities for certain countries. If your family is from Russia, there are charities that work to improve life in that country. There are charities for specific interests as well. If you like pets, horses, math, babies, nuns, dancers, trees, or hockey, there is most likely a charity that somehow improves life for people, animals, and organizations involved with those situations. For example, a charity could offer help to animals, or provide opportunities for people to participate in one of those activities. You can find a charity that works just in this country or a charity that does work all over the world. You can find one that has the same religious beliefs that you do. The choices really are limitless.

But what if you are interested in everything—pets, horses, math, babies, nuns, dancers, trees, *and* hockey? Can you find a charity for each of your interests and give money to all of them? You certainly can, but it might not be the best idea. Imagine that your grandpa split a $10 bill ten ways. He gave a dollar to you, a dollar to each of your two siblings, and a dollar to each of your seven cousins. You could each buy a candy bar with your money, but not much else. But what if your grandpa gave

The EVERYTHING KIDS' Money Book

the entire $10 to you? You could do a lot more with that money.

Donating to charity is similar. The more you split up your donations, the less effective your money will be in helping the causes you care about. You may have a very big heart and you may care about a lot of issues, but picking one or two that are the absolute most important lets you support your causes better.

How Do I Find a Charity for Me?

If you'd like to get involved with a charity but aren't sure how to find one, first make a list of your interests or concerns. Are you worried about the people who were affected by a recent earthquake or hurricane? Do you want to help find a cure for cancer? Does religion play an important role in your life and do you want to give money to a charity that puts what you've been taught into action? You might want to make sure other kids can have as good an education as you do, or you could be concerned about the effect of global warming on the polar bears.

If you're not really sure what you're interested in, you could take a look at some of the children's charities that help kids in different situations and locations—helping other kids might appeal to you. You might also want to think about local charities that you have some connection to. Your local museums are probably charities, and there are probably charities in your area that work to help feed or clothe needy people in your own community. You

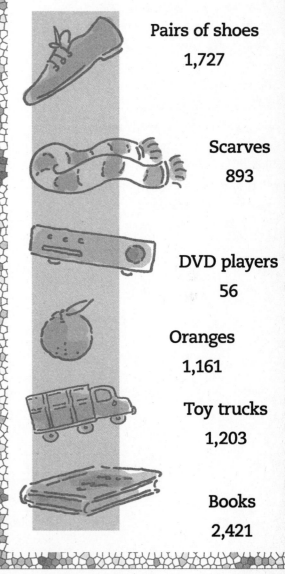

TOTAL TALLY

This charity has gotten its totals mixed up. Can you rearrange the numbers within each category to make the largest possible donation?

Pairs of shoes
1,727

Scarves
893

DVD players
56

Oranges
1,161

Toy trucks
1,203

Books
2,421

Dollars & Sense

Year Round Giving

Many people give a lot to charities at the holidays, but charities need money and donations all year round, and donations made at other times of the year can be very important. For example, donating your barely used sneakers in April to a charity that distributes them to kids in need will mean a child will have shoes to wear all summer.

can go to a website like Charity Navigator (*www.charitynavigator.org*) and type in your interests one at a time and read about the charities that are involved with them.

Once you decide on a cause, the next step is to do some research to find a charity that deals with your interests. Not all charities are alike. One of the biggest differences between charities is how much of the money they raise actually ends up being used directly for the people or cause they support. All charities need some money to help them run their business—to pay rent, employees, postage, advertising, and other costs. If you give $100 to a charity and $80 of it is used toward administrative costs, your money is not accomplishing as much as it would if you gave it to a charity that would use $95 to support your cause and only $5 on administrative costs. Charity Navigator can help you understand how the charities you are interested in use their money and help you make an educated choice.

Do Some Good: Giving to Charity

One of the easiest ways to get involved with charities is to donate money. You might decide you want to take a regular percentage of your allowance or earnings and donate it to the charity or charities of your choice. You might also decide to do some work just to earn money for charity. You could take a week and donate everything you earn walking dogs in your neighborhood to the SPCA (a charity that helps finds homes for pets). You could go through your neighborhood and ask people to give you their recyclable soda bottles and you could use the money from returning them to donate to the charity.

Another great way to regularly give money to charity is to put all your change in a jar and donate all of it to your favorite charity once a year. Or once in a while you can empty out your piggy bank and decide to donate

the money to charity. If you're going to donate cash, be sure to talk to your parents. They can help you make sure you know where and how to give your donation. You may need your parents to write a check, or you may need to be driven to a drop-off location.

There are likely to be lots of times when charities will ask you or your family for money. At Christmas, you will see Salvation Army workers ringing bells and asking for donations. At the grocery store, when your parents check out, the cashier may sometimes ask them if they want to donate $1 to a certain cause the store is helping to promote. You can also help charities by buying things from them. Your local hospital might sell Christmas cards and use the profits to help treat patients. A local charity organization might sell tulip bulbs to raise money.

Seeing Your Dollars at Work

Sometimes it can be hard to donate your hard-earned money and never really know where it has gone or how

PENNY FOR YOUR THOUGHTS

Why Do You Give?

Why do you want to be involved with charities? What makes you want to help other people? How does it make you feel when you do something charitable?

it has been used. There are some charities that help you see the good you've done. The Christian Children's Fund (*www.christianchildrensfund.org*) allows you to help one specific child in another country. You get updates and photos and can send letters to that child. Another great way to feel involved in your giving is to adopt an animal. You can "adopt" a wild animal through a variety of different charities (check out *www.wildlifeadoption.org* as examples). You make a donation and get a photo of your animal, as well as a certificate and sometimes even updates about your animal or its species. Some adoptions even offer a stuffed animal of your species to cuddle.

Other Donations

While cash is a great kind of donation, there are lots of other donations you can make that can help people. Many charities accept donations of used clothing, toys, games, books, and other household items. They might distribute these items to people in need or sell them and use the money raised for the charity.

Sometimes you can donate things you don't need or want and make a big difference in someone's life. The Lion's Club is a charity that accepts donations of used eyeglasses, which they refurbish and give to those in need. If you wear glasses and get a new pair, you have no need for the old pair and the Lion's Club makes sure they help someone else see.

You can also donate new items to charities. Your local food bank always needs donations of nonperishable food, such as canned or dry goods. There are organizations that collect school supplies, personal hygiene items (toothpaste, toothbrushes, soap, and so on), and more to give to hospital patients, needy schools, and soldiers.

WORK FOR THE CAUSE

Giving money and goods to charities is an important way to help out and make a difference in people's lives, but

WORDS to KNOW

VOLUNTEER: A volunteer is a person who donates his or her time to a charity to do work for them.

you can help out in other ways. Charities need volunteers to do many things. You could help paint their offices, organize items that are donated, address envelopes for letters asking for donations, recycle their garbage, clean out animal's cages (such as at an animal shelter), or wrap gifts that have been donated for needy kids.

There are many simple ways you can work for charity all on your own at home. You can make cards for patients at veteran's hospitals, write letters to child patients at hospitals, or draw pictures and send them to a local nursing home. These small gestures can mean a lot to the people who receive them! You can also participate in charity walks or runs where you get people to sponsor you. Your sponsors agree to pay the charity a certain amount for every mile you walk. The farther you go, the more you earn!

Some kids hold special events to raise money for charity all on their own. One popular type is a Muscular Dystrophy Association (MDA) Carnival. MDA is an organization that funds research and treatment for muscular dystrophy, a serious disease that causes muscle weakness. The MDA has a website, *www.mdacarnivals. com*, that explains how to set up and run a carnival that will benefit the MDA.

Other kids set up lemonade stands to provide money to charities. One girl has a website about her that explains how she did it and how you can, too: *www .alexslemonade.org*.

JOIN ME!

While one person can make a difference, the more people you can involve in charity, the greater the impact you can have. Some charities have programs where families can volunteer together. Your family could work to build a new home for a needy family or help serve homeless people dinner at a shelter. Many charities require that child volunteers have adult supervision. If

Dollars & Sense

Giving It All Away
You might get so inspired by the charity you are interested in that you want to give them all of your money. It's great to want to help, but if you gave away all your money, you might someday end up needing charity yourself. Instead, pick a percent of your income or savings you want to donate and also be sure to volunteer your time.

TRY THIS

Give the Gift of Giving
If you have someone that is hard to buy holiday gifts for (like a grandparent or aunt who has everything), you can make a donation to a charity in that person's name as your gift. There's no shopping and you both have the satisfaction of knowing your gift has done some good in the world.

GENEROUS WITH WORDS

Charity comes in many forms and has many

Not an amateur + movies before DVDs – O _____

The first 4 letters of VOLUME + N + STEER without the S _____

names. Can you figure out these different words

that all have to do with "giving"?

A greeting – LO + first half of PERSON _____

GENERAL – AL + the middle 3 letters of HOUSE _____

Tasty treat with a hole in it – UT + the last 3 letters of DATE _____

Give a hand + FUEL without the E _____

you belong to a scout troop or a church youth organization, your leader can organize volunteer work for the group and provide the supervision.

Working together with friends or family to do good can be a great way to have fun and feel like you are making a difference. The more people you involve, the greater the projects that you can take on.

The best way to get your group interested in a project is to collect some information about the charity and how you can help them. Find out how much time would be involved and what kind of goal you should have for your project. Then present the idea to your group with all of the details.

In addition to getting family and friends involved with charity, there are lots of ways that large corporations or even small local companies can help. There are many companies that give a portion of their profits to charity. You may see products that have printed on their packaging "a portion of the proceeds from this product go to" and then the name of a charity. There are websites such as *www.igive.com* where your family can do online shopping and have a portion of the profit from their purchase go to a charity of their choice.

There are also websites that will donate money or goods to charity if you just visit the site. For example, *www.freerice.org* donates rice when people visit the site and take a free vocabulary quiz. Opportunities like these allow you and your family to get involved and help make sure money and goods are donated to charities.

Schools Can Help Too!

Schools are a great place to encourage charitable giving. There are a lot of great projects that work well for schools. Collections of donations of coats, books, and canned food are common. Schools are also a great place to organize volunteers. If you want to get your school involved in a charity, you'll need permission from your teacher or principal. You can get just your class involved, or you can coordinate an event that involves the entire school. If you want to get the whole school involved, present an idea to your student council and see if they would be interested in organizing it. If you're interested in something that your class is learning about, your teacher may let you bring in a bin for donated items or allow you to pass out fliers to your classmates.

Some schools choose one charity to support for an entire year. If you have a charity that appeals to you, present it to the principal as a possibility for next year. Organizations within your school may be interested in contributing to charities as well. If there is a school band, orchestra, chorus, or sports team, you could ask the organization to sponsor your charity and take it on as their special cause.

Fun Fact

We Work

Many Americans—44 percent—do some volunteer work. If all those volunteers were paid for their time, the grand total would come to $240 billion a year.

$

PENNY FOR YOUR THOUGHTS

Why Charity?
Why do you think we need to have charities? How would we need to change our country and the world so that they would not be necessary?

Appendix A
GLOSSARY

ADMINISTRATIVE COSTS
the money a charity spends on running its business instead of directly helping people or its cause

ALLOWANCE
an amount of money paid regularly

ASSET
anything owned that can be converted into cash to cover your debt

BANK NOTE
a promise by a bank that a person could exchange the paper note for gold or silver

BARTER
to exchange or trade items of value

BENEFITS
something of value an employee receives as part of his or her job that has a money value

BLANK
an unmarked piece of metal in the shape and size of a finished coin

BROKER
a person who buys and sells stocks for customers

BUDGET
a plan for how to spend and save your money

BULLION
gold or silver in bar form

CD
certificate of deposit; a type of savings account

CHARITY
an organization that raises or collects money or goods to help other people or certain causes

CHECK
a written note that is a substitute for cash, allowing the bearer to exchange it for cash at the bank

COMMODITY
an item that is traded and has a universal value

COUNTERFEIT
fake money

COURIER
messenger

CREDIT
an agreement between a buyer and seller where the buyer leaves with something and agrees to pay for it later

CURRENCY
objects like metal or paper that are recognized as money

DENOMINATION
a unit of value in currency; for example, 1 cent, 5 cents, $1

DEPOSIT
money put into a bank

DIE
a tool for stamping out the design of a coin

DIME
a U.S. coin worth ten cents

DISME
a dime

DIVERSIFICATION
to invest money in a wide variety of companies or industries

DIVIDEND
a share of earnings paid to investors in a company

ECONOMY
a country's system of earning and spending

ELECTRONIC FUNDS TRANSFER (EFT)
transferring money online

ENTREPRENEUR
someone who sets up a business

EQUITY
a homeowner's ownership value in a home

EXCHANGES
places where stocks are bought and sold

FEDERAL RESERVE SYSTEM (THE FED)
the central bank of the United States

529 PLAN
an investment account that is tax-free and which can only be used to pay for education

FUND MANAGER
a person who controls a mutual fund and selects different stocks for it to own

IMPULSE BUYING
purchasing something on the spur of the moment without thinking it through and making an educated decision

INFLATION
a change in the value of money when prices go up

INTAGLIO PRINTING
a printing process that uses an engraved plate

INTEREST
an amount charged for the use of money

LEGEND
the words on a coin

LOAN
an agreement where one person borrows money from another and agrees to pay it back later

LOSS
a negative amount of income; spending more on expenses than you earn

LOTTERY
state-run games of chance people enter hoping to win money

MARKET SURVEY
a study that determines if there is a need for a business in your area

MINTING
the process of creating a coin out of metal

MORTGAGE
a loan to buy a home

MOTTO
a brief statement that usually expresses an ideal or goal

MUTUAL FUND
a group of people (investors) pooling their money to invest in a group of stocks, bonds, and other securities

NICKEL
a U.S. coin worth five cents

NONPROFIT AGENCY
a charity that works to help people or a cause and does not earn any money itself

OBVERSE
the front of a coin

ON-US CHECKS
a check drawn on one bank which is deposited at the same bank

ORGANIC
food grown without any chemicals

PASSBOOK ACCOUNT
a savings account that has a small book in which all transactions are recorded

PENNY
a U.S. coin worth one cent

PROFIT
money earned from a business after expenses

PROMISSORY NOTE
a written promise to pay someone

QUARTER
a U.S. coin worth 25 cents

REEDING
ridges around the edge of a coin

RENT
monthly payments in exchange for being able to live in a house or apartment

REVERSE
the back of a coin

SECRET SERVICE
a branch of the Department of the Treasury in charge of finding and capturing counterfeiters; it also provides protection for the president and his or her family

SECURITIES AND EXCHANGE COMMISSION (SEC)
a governmental department that oversees the businesses that sell stocks and also handles customer complaints

SPECULATOR
a person who enters into a risky business to make fast money

STANDARD
a measure by which something can be compared and judged

STATEMENT ACCOUNT
a type of savings account that sends you a statement each month with a list of transactions

STOCK
a share of a business that can be bought and sold

STRIKE
to impress a design on; this comes from the days when coins were actually struck using a hammer

TAX RETURN
a document you file with the government that shows how much money you must pay in taxes

TAXES
money that people pay the government so it can provide public services

TRANSFER
to move money from one account to another

TRANSIT CHECK
a check written on one bank, which is deposited in another

TUITION
a fee paid to attend a school

UNDERWRITE
to take on financial responsibility for all or part of a business

UNEMPLOYED
a person without a job who is looking for work

VALUE
an item's worth

VOLUNTEER
a person who donates his or her time to a charity

WITHDRAWAL
removing money from an account

WITHHOLDING
taxes taken out of your pay by your employer and paid directly to the government

Appendix B
RESOURCES

BOOKS

Berenstain, Stan and Jan Berenstain, *The Berenstain Bears' The Trouble with Money* (Random House, 1983)

Erlbach, Arlene, *The Kids' Business Book* (Lerner, 1998)

Fukomoto, Jodi, *Fun Money Folds for Kids* (Island Heritage, 2005)

Karlitz, Gail, *Growing Money: A Complete Investing Guide for Kids* (Price Stern Sloan, 2001)

Kiefer, Jeanne, *Jobs for Kids* (Millbrook, 2003)

Lewis, Barbara A., *The Kid's Guide to Service Projects: Over 500 Service Ideas for Young People Who Want to Make a Difference* (Free Spirit, 1995)

Mandelberg, Robert, *Tricks with Dollar Bills: Another Way to Make Your Money Disappear* (Sterling, 2006)

Nathan, Amy and Debbie Palen, *The Kids' Allowance Book* (Backinprint, 2006)

Nguyen, Duy, *Paper Airplanes with Dollar Bills: Another Way to Throw Your Money Away* (Sterling, 2005)

Parker, Nancy Winslow, *Money, Money, Money: The Meaning of the Art and Symbols on United States Paper Currency* (HarperCollins Children's Books, 1995)

Sabin, Ellen, *The Giving Book* (Watering Can, 2004)

Standish, David, *The Art of Money* (Chronicle Books, 2000)

Tucker, Tom, *Brainstorm! The Stories of Twenty American Kid Investors* (Farrar, Straus and Giroux, 1998)

WEBSITES

ALEX'S LEMONADE STAND
Learn how to set up a lemonade stand to benefit charity.
www.alexslemonade.org

THE ALLOWANCE ROOM
Find out how much you need to earn and save for items you're longing for.
www.cibc.com/ca/youth/under-12/allowance-room/allowance-room.html

THE AMERICAN NUMISMATIC ASSOCIATION
This coin collector's organization website has tons of information about coin collecting.
www.money.org

CHARITY NAVIGATOR
This site helps you locate and evaluate charities you might be interested in.
www.charitynavigator.org

FREE RICE
Taking a quick vocabulary quiz on this site results in a donation of rice to the needy.
www.freerice.org

IGIVE.COM
Profits from purchases your family makes online at this site are donated to the charity of your choice.
www.igive.com

INFLATION CALCULATOR
Use this to find out how much an amount spent in the past is worth today.
✍www.bls.gov/cpi

KIDS BANK
Learn about money facts with characters like Penny and Dollar Bill.
✍www.kidsbank.com

LEARNING BANK
Information for kids about the Federal Deposit Insurance Corporation.
✍www.fdic.gov/about/learn/learning/index.html

MDA CARNIVALS
Learn how to hold a carnival to benefit the Muscular Dystrophy Association.
✍www.mdacarnivals.com

MONEYFACTORY.ORG
The Bureau of Engraving and Printing's site has lots of cool facts and games.
✍www.moneyfactory.org

MONEYOPOLIS.ORG
Play an entertaining and engaging game about money on this site.
✍www.moneyopolis.org

PET COST BUDGET
Find out how much it will really cost to add that puppy or kitten to your family with this list of costs.
✍www.spca.bc.ca/animalcare/petcost.asp

SENSE AND DOLLARS
Take some cool money quizzes and find out how much you really know.
✍www.senseanddollars.thinkport.org

WEBKINZ
Register your Webkinz stuffed animal and earn virtual dollars you can spend on the site.
✍www.webkinz.com

WHAT DO YOU LIKE?
Learn what kinds of jobs you might be interested in, how to get there, and how much they earn.
✍www.bls.gov/k12

WHERE'S GEORGE?
This site allows you to track where dollar bills have been.
✍www.wheresgeorge.com

WILDLIFE ADOPTION
This site lets you adopt wild animals to make a difference in their lives.
✍www.wildlifeadoption.org

WISE POCKETS
Learn how to manage your money, play games, and print cool stuff.
✍www.wisepockets.org

Appendix C
PUZZLE ANSWERS

Island Hopping • page 5

Space Trade • page 12

Gronk will get 4 Kerplinks.

Woozzee will get 30 Splotz.

Coin Hunt • page 18

Money Memories • page 22

Billfold • page 35

BILLBOARD
BILLION
BILLIARDS
BILLOW

SCAFFOLD
UNFOLD
TWOFOLD
BLINDFOLD

Seal It Up • page 37

Copper Counterfeit • page 27

The EVERYTHING KIDS Money Book

Mock Up Money • page 43

HAND
CLEAR
MONEY
TIME
PRINTER
FOUND

NCROETIETFU = COUNTERFEIT

Do You Have Change for a Cow? • page 51

Multiply 7 pigs x 2 = 14

Subtract 3 cows = 11

Add 6 geese = 17

Subract 7 pigs = 10

Add 6 sheep = 16

Cereal Serial • page 45

Initially Yours • page 58

Savings Account Withdrawal and Deposit: SAWD

Saturday or Weekends Only: SOWO

Interest-Free Deposit Account: IFDA

Inside For Daily Account Information: IFDAI

Long-Term Loan: LTL

Legal Trade Union: LTU

NSF stands for Non-Sufficient Funds

Charge It! • page 61

interest

penalty

bank

loan

money

borrowed

Twins or Not • page 71

Payback Time • page 69

Work and Play • page 73

```
R   T A S     W F R
A T I D T G H O A P B L B
  R S D A R A L N I R O R
B A S E B A L L G L O V E
I D U D L D E O E L K E A
T E E   E E   W R O E L T
        S       W N Y H
```

Attack the Tax • page 83

Millionaire's Birthday • page 98

wallets

check

coins

money belts

paper money

purses

credit cards

Future Finances • page 95

2 x $3 = $6.00

$7 + $3 = $10.00

2 x $2 = $4.00

$6 + 50 cents = $6.50

3 x $3 = $9.00

half a dollar = 50 cents

90 cents + 9 cents = 99 cents

2 x $1.00 = $2.00

Quirky Collector • page 102

Splash Money • page 107

PayLittle costs the least.

PayLittle: $21.50

BuyMore: $22

SpendLess: $22.50

Baffling Banks • page 113

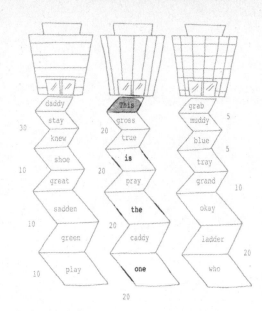

Julie's mortgage is $80.

Add Up Dinner • page 108

The total is $7. Allen has enough for dinner.

Budget Beth • page 120

Beth needs to budget $7 each week. The three missing totals are $21, $42, and $56

The EVERYTHING KIDS® Money Book

How Much Is It? • page 123

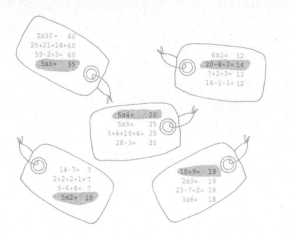

Dare to Compare • page 126

The cheapest is the $65 item because the $7 tax isn't added in.

Boxed Surprises • page 129

Total Tally • page 131

Pairs of shoes = 7,721

Scarves = 983

DVD players = 65

Oranges = 6,111

Toy trucks = 3,210

Books = 4,221

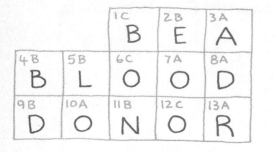

To get in the room you open A DOOR.
Another word for mix is BLEND.
What a ghost says: BOO!

Generous with Words • page 136

The first 4 letters of VOLUME + N + STEER without the S = VOLUNTEER

Not an amateur + movies before DVDs – O = PROVIDE

A greeting – LO + first half of PERSON = HELPER

Tasty treat with a hole in it – UT + the last 3 letters of DATE = DONATE

GENERAL – AL + the middle 3 letters of HOUSE = GENEROUS

Give a hand + FUEL without the E = HELPFUL